DEAF
Again

::

Fourth Edition

::

Mark Drolsbaugh

Deaf Again

Published by:
Handwave Publications
1121 Bethlehem Pike # 60-134
Springhouse, PA 19477

Website: www.handwavepublications.com

Cover design and layout courtesy of
Yvonne Vermillion, Magic Graphix

ISBN-13: 978-0-9657460-6-9

Library of Congress Control Number:
2007905600

Dedication

::

*In loving memory of Linda Baine,
who actually taught me how to be Deaf.*

*In loving memory of Martin J. Bronenberg,
my grandfather and the most inspiring
mentor of them all.*

*In loving memory of Dr. Francine White,
who mastered the art of empowering people
to accomplish their dreams.*

Acknowledgments

$$\vdots$$

Heartfelt thanks to my parents and grandparents, for all the love and support.
To my wife Melanie, for putting up with all the insanity.
To Darren, Brandon,and Lacey, love and laughter personified.
To our family and friends in Canada.

To Teresa Coates, Marvin Miller, Damara Goff Paris, Lisa Bain, Sam Scott, Michael P. Ralph, Patty Saar, Lisa Santomen Hellberg, Stephanie Smith,Dolly Schulman, and Trudy Suggs. All of you, in your own unique way, have helped make this book happen.

To Yvonne Vermillion at Magic Graphix for her creative and technical expertise with the layout, cover, and website design.
To Chuck Vermillion at HelpPublish.com for his keen insight and editorial assistance.

To the Gallaudet University Department of Counseling, Graduate School and Professional Programs: Clearly one of the best educational experiences in the world.

To Colby Tecklin, Jaime Eustace-Tecklin, Neil McDevitt, and Sarah McDevitt: See you on Friday.

To Jeff Jones, Vijay Advani, Derek Gambrell and Jason McKinnie: As always, We're The Family.

i

Introduction

∴

The hardest fight a man has to fight is to live in a
world where every single day someone is trying to make
you someone you do not want to be---

e.e. cummings

One of the hardest fights a deaf man has to fight is
to live in a world where every single day someone
is trying to make him hear. When your audiogram is
free-falling towards the depths of profound deafness,
the quest for the world of sound can be very difficult, if
not impossible.

As a hearing youngster who gradually went hard
of hearing and eventually deaf, I struggled all the way
through my high school years. I did everything I could to
hang on to my hearing persona. What makes this really
odd is the fact that the whole time this charade was going
on, Deaf culture was always there for me, right under
my nose; both my parents are deaf.

But as quickly as I was born into Deaf culture, I
was taken away from it. When my hearing loss was
initially diagnosed, medical professionals took an entirely
pathological approach. They emphasized hearing aids
and speech therapy, and that was it. Since they did not
recognize or understand Deaf culture, they frowned upon
the use of sign language. They preached a skewed version
of the old *it's a hearing world* philosophy. Somehow, they
convinced not only my hearing relatives, but also my deaf
parents that sign language should not be used in my
presence. It was a vain attempt to hold on to what little
residual hearing and speech I had left. This experience left
me with the impression that deafness was a horrendous

condition that needed to be fixed, or at least covered up. Consequently, I felt obligated to spend the next several years of my life trying to pass myself off as a hearing person. I spent those years living my life as someone I thought I should be, instead of who I really was.

Inevitably, I would wake up. A series of fateful events turned my life around to the point where I realized that it was okay to be deaf. It took twenty-three years to come to this realization, twenty-three years of struggling with my identity. Instead of trying to deny or fix deafness, I found that I could be deaf again, so I grew tremendously from these experiences. As opposed to *overcoming* deafness, this book expresses the joys of *finding* deafness.

While putting together a rough draft of what eventually became this book, I also noticed that a number of spiritual issues repeatedly surfaced. I began to realize that in its own strange way, deafness has been a spiritual blessing. Dealing with deafness can be a struggle at times, I won't deny that. But it's also a struggle that allows one to search for meaning in life from a unique perspective. An old Zen saying applies here: *Empty your cup so that it may be filled.* Deafness emptied my cup. The void in one area of my life allowed me to have enriching experiences in others. *Deaf Again* is thus a deeply introspective account of the challenges faced in coming to terms with hearing loss.

As you will see in the upcoming chapters, there is no etched-in-stone definition of "deaf"; there is simply too much diversity out there. There are deaf people who consider themselves culturally Deaf (caps intended), embracing American Sign Language as their own language. Then there are the oralists, deaf people who favor speech over sign language. There are also those who are somewhat in-between, using whatever combination of speech and sign language they are comfortable with. All of these people have incredibly diverse backgrounds: Deaf people who went to residential schools; deaf people who went to mainstream schools that had specialized programs for deaf students; deaf people who went to hearing schools alone, without any deaf peers or assistance; deaf people who are prelingually deaf, hard of hearing, or late-deafened. There are deaf people with hearing parents, and deaf people with deaf parents. All of these people may have varying opinions of what deafness means.

What makes *Deaf Again* unique is the fact that I have personally experienced deafness from many perspectives: as a hearing toddler, as a hard-of-hearing child, as a deaf adolescent, and as a culturally Deaf adult. Throughout all of this, I saw firsthand the philosophical war of culture versus pathology. This book is intended to give you an up-close look at each viewpoint, as seen through the eyes of someone who has been on both sides of the fence. Whatever your own background may be, I hope that you can find stories that you can relate to, and stories that you can learn from. So sit back, empty your cup, and enjoy the journey.

Prologue

::

It was another dreary Saturday morning, and as always I was stocking the shelves in the supermarket where I worked part-time. I hated the Saturday morning shift because it often meant getting up at five-thirty a.m. with a throbbing hangover. Nearly every weekend I would find myself in the same predicament: My college friends would stop by on Friday night, raving about a great party I couldn't afford to miss. I'd politely decline, citing my responsibilities at work the next day. They, in turn, would cite my responsibilities as a beer-chugging party animal.

Somehow, what they said made sense. I'd cave in and go along with them. Then they would proceed to have a great time—and I would pretend to. After all, I was as deaf as a post and had no idea of what was going on. Sure, with my residual hearing and respectable speech ability I managed to pull off a few one-on-one conversations. Unfortunately, group discussions were an exercise in futility and it wouldn't be long before I would get bored out of my mind.

Out of this boredom I would always wind up reaching for more beers. I'd routinely out-drink my friends. By midnight, I would have one hell of a buzz. By three a.m. I would be flat-out drunk. By four a.m., I would be crawling into bed (if I made it that far). By six-thirty, I would be cursing under my breath as I punched in for work.

This particular Saturday was no different. Saturday was diaper day, when a whole truckload of diapers would get dropped off at the store in the wee hours of the morning. These diapers were waiting for me when I trudged in with bloodshot eyes and a pounding headache.

1

As I loaded them onto a cart to be wheeled out and packed on the shelves, it felt like the veins in my head were going to burst.

By nine a.m. the diapers were done and it was time to do the really mundane stuff. I worked in the general merchandise section, ordering and packing out non-perishable goods such as school supplies, personal hygiene products, hardware, toys, and various clothing items. Each time I worked a shift, there were always customers who needed help finding certain products in the store. I didn't mind the interruptions so long as they were from regular customers who knew me. On the other hand, I absolutely dreaded having to talk to new customers who didn't understand that I was deaf. It was always an awkward experience. The regulars knew me well enough to make sure they spoke clearly, and I was familiar with their speech patterns after seeing the same faces every week for three years.

The new customers were almost always an adventure of foul-ups, bleeps, and blunders. One man repeatedly asked where he could find a certain product, and he began to shout in my ear when I told him I was deaf. I never got to explain that he needed to look me in the eye and enunciate his words more clearly for me to lip-read—because he stormed off, muttering angrily. Another man, whose question I successfully understood and answered, asked me what country I was from. Apparently, I had an interesting accent. When I told him that it was just a result of my not being able to hear my voice because I was deaf, his eyes widened. "Oh," he said, backing away. "I see." He nodded awkwardly, waved goodbye, and made a hasty retreat. From this experience I learned to simply say, "Excuse me, I'm a bit hard of hearing. Could you speak a little slower, please?" This always got a favorable response. For whatever reason, the word "deaf" seemed to freak people out.

And then, there were people who freaked *me* out. On one occasion, I had turned around just in time to see a woman in the middle of a hissy fit.

"Why, I never . . . (unintelligible) . . . such a rude man . . . (unintelligible) . . . I oughta. . . ." I could only shrug in bewilderment. Ten minutes later, this woman returned with the store manager and pointed in my direction. The manager smiled, made a comment or two, and all of a sudden this woman grabbed my arm and apologized profusely.

"I'm *so* sorry! I didn't know you were *death*." Apparently, she thought I was ignoring her when she asked me a question behind my back. She just couldn't see that I was *death*. At least I liked her better than the guy with the walrus mustache. Nothing, except perhaps grabbing him in a headlock and shaving the fur off his face, could have helped in this situation. I explained to him that I couldn't hear, and he patiently repeated his question slowly several times. Unfortunately, the rug on his upper lip effectively camouflaged every single word. In exasperation, I just sighed and said, "Aisle twenty-seven." Never mind that there were only twenty-six aisles in the store. It was his problem. Let *him* figure it out.

But today, there was one customer who would change everything. My attitude, my confidence, my job, my future, my life, *everything*. I was stocking the shelves with dental floss when someone politely tapped me on the shoulder. I turned around thinking, *what is it now*—and was very surprised to find it was a woman asking me something in fluent sign language.

"Hi, I'm Linda Baine. Remember me?" Indeed I did. She worked at the Pennsylvania School for the Deaf, and I remembered meeting her when she had interpreted a community event a few years earlier. Linda was a hearing woman, but she signed so smoothly she looked deaf herself. It was such a relief to be able to converse effortlessly with someone after all those adventures with the other customers.

"Sure, I remember you," I said. "How have you been doing?"

3

"Just great," Linda began. "I just got promoted to Coordinator of Residential Education, which is why I'm here. Listen, we have an opening for a dorm supervisor at the school. I'm telling you, this would be the *perfect* opportunity for you."

My life would never, ever be the same.

1

::

On the afternoon of October 12th, 1966, a very pregnant Sherry Drolsbaugh was wheeled into the delivery room accompanied by her husband, Don. They strapped her in—yes, they really tied her down—and ignored her scream for morphine. Whether that was common practice back then, or if they thought my mother was a mental patient, I have no idea. This took place at the Albert Einstein Medical Center near downtown Philadelphia. It was one of the best hospitals in the city. But whatever skills the doctors had back in the 1960s, even the best of them knew very little about deafness. For my mother and father, both deaf, this set the stage for a harrowing experience.

As Sherry was strapped down, she gestured to one of the nurses. She wanted the nurse to free one of her hands. This way, she explained, she would be able to communicate with her husband via sign language. Presumably, she would use that hand to tell him what a bastard he was for getting her in this mess in the first place. Good sport that he is, Don stuck with her throughout the entire ordeal.

And what an ordeal it was. Right off the bat there were some, uh, technical difficulties. As Sherry explains it, the nurse took a needle that was to administer the epidural and applied it to her backside. It was taped on so that it would continuously administer some much-needed pain relief. But as the whole drama unfolded, Sherry constantly complained that she was in pain. One of the nurses, getting in close for a good view, leaned on Sherry's leg. Needless to say, Sherry was not amused.

"Tell the nurse to get her elbow off me!" she barked. When Don informed the nurse of Sherry's discomfort, the nurse shook her head and chuckled. She insisted there was no way Sherry could feel anything, what with the epidural and all.

The hospital staff kept working and Sherry eventually gave birth, screaming bloody murder the whole time. Finally, when the doctor began fixing up my poor mother so that she'd be on the road to recovery from this memorable experience, she just couldn't take it anymore. She repeatedly complained about the excruciating pain. She begged the doctor to knock her out with a good old-fashioned general anesthetic to help her get through this agony. Sighing, the doctor figured, why not? Might as well help her relax. Might as well get her to shut up, too. Everyone would be happy.

Unfortunately, this whole caper was far from over. As the anesthesia mask was placed over her nose and mouth, Sherry's eyes widened in horror. Gasping for air, she realized there wasn't any. Yep, that's right, no air at all. She was suffocating. Overcome with panic, Sherry waved vigorously at the doctor and attending nurses. But since Sherry is prelingually deaf, she'd never had the ability to speak clearly—it was a communication barrier that almost turned deadly. The doctor and nurses just assumed that Sherry was one of those difficult, high-maintenance patients. They simply ignored her muffled grunts and frantic struggling. They smiled, reassuring Sherry that everything was okay, and told her to just let the anesthetic do its work. They further restrained her and kept the mask firmly in place. In horror, my mother realized she was in a nightmare of a situation one would expect to find on *The Twilight Zone*.

Thinking quickly, Sherry raised the one hand that the nurse had freed a little bit earlier and anxiously started fingerspelling to Don:

"N-o a-i-r! N-o a-i-r!"

Alarmed and confused, Don looked around the operating room and saw that the anesthesia machine wasn't working. A pump that was supposed to be pumping wasn't pumping. It was clamped shut, stuck in place. Don grabbed the mask off Sherry's face and pointed out the defective equipment to the doctor, who gasped in both shock and embarrassment. He apologized and asked Sherry to "just hang in there" while he finished up. The whole thing was almost over. Besides, all screw-ups notwithstanding, my folks were overjoyed to be the proud new parents of a healthy baby boy.

When Sherry was ready to be sent back to her room, a nurse helped her off the delivery room table and eased her onto a gurney. Immediately, the nurse spotted something on the table and gasped. There was a large wet spot in the vicinity of the needle that was (supposedly) administering the epidural. Peeling off the tape that was holding the needle in place, the nurse found that it was bent off at an angle. It had been leaking onto the table the whole time instead of providing Sherry the painkilling relief she begged for. No wonder she'd been screaming the whole time.

Sherry noticed the look on the nurse's face and started to panic. *What could it possibly be now?* She asked Don and the nurse what was wrong.

"Nothing at all, nothing at all, and the baby is just fine," replied the nurse, speaking slowly so my parents could read her lips. Turning to Don, she said, "Your wife is a very brave woman. She just had a natural childbirth, whether she knew it or not." Oh, she knew. Believe me, she knew.

2

::

From that zany childbirth all the way up to the first grade, I had perfectly normal hearing. I was able to acquire language the way all hearing children normally do, through both auditory and visual input. I could have conversations on the phone with my hearing grandparents, and seemed to interact normally with other children my age. I attended kindergarten at the Henry H. Houston School in Philadelphia and initially there was nothing out of the ordinary that anyone could have noticed.

Slowly and ever so subtly, "normal" went out the window. Something wasn't right. I got confused at times during weekly music classes but couldn't figure out why. There were moments when I felt something was out of whack whenever we sang songs together. When it was my or my group's turn to sing a line, I either missed my cue or babbled something incomprehensible. Sometimes I even made up my own lines. I would sing about my gal who rode the boat outdoors with Al and Louie, and then I would wonder why everyone was looking at me so funny. I would shrug bewilderedly as the teacher corrected me; the actual words, she said, were "Michael row the boat ashore, hallelujah." Hey, I was only singing what I thought I had heard. At that age, children are naturally egocentric; I couldn't help but think that the other kids were receiving the same warped input as I was. I didn't really believe at the time that something might be seriously wrong with me.

Finally, my weirdness was exposed for all to see on one fateful day in the first grade. It was time for our favorite weekly activity, Show 'n' Tell. As did any other student, I loved this part of class because it put me in the spotlight and allowed me to share my toys with everyone. This time, however, I was doomed. For some reason, my teacher decided to have one huge Show 'n' Tell activity featuring two first grade classes working together. Instead of a cozy atmosphere of twelve or so students, there were thirty kids packed into one big room. I felt lost. It was my first experience of complete disorientation. I realized that I had no idea of what anyone was saying, and wondered how I would know when it was my turn. But the worst was yet to come.

"Mark... you're up," said my teacher, Ms. Brown.

"Huh?"

"Mark, it's your turn. Come on up." I made my way up to the front, bringing the toy I knew would knock 'em dead: My GI Joe doll, dressed up in army fatigues. I even took good measure to toughen him up for class. I had seared off part of his scalp with a lit match, cut some scars into his face with a knife, and had thrown him around in the dirt; anything for that rugged look. Hey, I wanted my GI Joe to look *tough*. No one would mess with him, and I would impress the class.

Immediately, though, I was in trouble. I started by explaining how GI Joe had survived several bombings, knife fights, attacks by hairy savages, and even that yecchy tea party thrown by the girl with the Barbie set. Whatever the danger, Joe always got out alive. Then, suddenly, a hand was raised. One of the kids had a question, and it was a kid from the other first grade class. I had no idea who he was. Apparently, since I didn't know him, I wasn't familiar with his speech pattern. There was no way I could understand what he was saying in a crowded classroom, all those rows back. Thus began my coming out party, where all notions that I was a hearing boy went out the window.

"Where did you blsszth thsdke klsnolthng?"

"What?" I responded.

9

"Where'dublsthes tsjdkke gsjdngfhg?"

"WHAT??" I was getting frustrated. At this juncture, Ms. Brown cut in to point out that my manners were inappropriate. She tried to explain that instead of contorting my face and screaming, "WHAT??", it would be more gentlemanly to politely raise my eyebrows and say "yes?" to the boy.

"Yes, what?" I asked Ms. Brown.

"Don't say what, say yes."

"WHAT?"

"Y-E-S. Yes."

"What was the question I'm saying yes to?"

"No, no... you say 'yes?' politely to him so he'll repeat the question." Shrugging, I looked back at the boy.

"Yes?"

"Where did blshdth thesjcl dlnfjthng?"

"WHAT????"

And so the verbal volleyball went on. I had no real understanding of what was happening, and no idea of the implications behind this drama. I only remember the wide-eyed looks I got from the whole classroom. *Something* was not right, but at this young age, I was unable to grasp the fact that I was going deaf.

Shortly after the Show 'n' Tell fiasco, I found myself in my grandparents' apartment. Back in those days, the word "accessibility" didn't exist. There was no effective communication between the school and my deaf parents. Anytime a phone call had to be made, teachers would call my maternal grandparents, Martin and Rose, because they could hear. Inadvertently, for better and for worse, they wound up taking charge of my educational progress (or lack thereof).

On this infamous day, my grandfather summoned me and asked me to sit down. He seemed a bit anxious and I still remember quite vividly the worried look of concern on his face. Apparently, he must have received one of those good news/bad news phone calls from my teacher. The good news was, "No, we don't think your

10

grandson is crazy after all." The bad news was, "Instead, we think he has a significant hearing loss."

It was time for the truth to come out. My grandfather started with small talk, nothing out of the ordinary. Then, suddenly, he asked what seemed to be an unusual question:

"Can you understand what I'm saying?"

"Yeah, sure..." I was perplexed. I couldn't see what the big deal was, and yet he looked so *worried*.

"Okay, now let's try it this way." My grandfather lifted his hand, covered his mouth, and spoke again.

"Howbout rhynow? Cnu erwt imsyng? Mrk, cnu unrandme?"

"What? Yes?"

My grandfather recoiled in shock. Reality struck, and it struck hard. I'd been reading lips all along. Up until that point, my residual hearing and speaking ability were just enough to cover up any indication of a hearing loss. Not anymore.

Now this is where it gets complicated. That one simple discovery, and the reaction to it, had a major impact on the path my life would take. For the first time, I understood that something was seriously wrong, *and that something was seriously wrong with me.* Let me make it clear, if it isn't already, that my grandparents both loved me so much they would do anything to make my life as enjoyable and successful as possible. At the same time, there was a paradox—a paradox that I would not come to understand until more than twenty years later.

Fast-forward several years for just a moment here: It wasn't until I took a Psycho-social Aspects of Deafness course at Gallaudet University that I finally understood what had happened when my grandparents discovered I was going deaf. (Doctors confirmed my grandfather's worst fears when they diagnosed a progressive sensorineural hearing loss.) My teacher described what is known as *The Diagnostic Crisis* of deafness. When hearing parents (in my case, grandparents) first learn that their child is deaf,

11

it can be very overwhelming. It is a shock, a tremendous shock, and it sets off a reaction that is similar to the stages of grief (shock, denial, anger, depression, the whole works). The difference is, they are not grieving a dead person. They are grieving for someone who is very much alive, and in the process can greatly influence that person.

When a deaf child sees his hearing family react negatively over his or her newly diagnosed deafness, a lasting impression is made. Since the parents are visibly upset and ship the kid off to every medical specialist they can find—even with the best intentions of finding a miracle cure—the child may perceive a different message:

Deafness is bad. I am deaf. I need to be fixed. I must be like them, no matter what, because deaf is bad.

The irony is, my grandparents were doing everything in their power to help me. They sent me to doctors, audiologists, speech therapists, everything but a witch doctor. Their actions on a surface level were saying, "We love you and we'll do anything we can to help you hear." Unbeknownst to them, the mixed message I received was, "We love you, but deafness is a horrible condition. You've got to be fixed."

What are the psychological implications of such a message? To me, it meant I had to deny who I really was, and that somehow I had to pretend that I could hear. It meant I had to brown-nose hearing people, act like them, act like I understood them, and remove myself from anything associated with deafness. In other words, sign language was *verboten*. I was told not to sign and I respectfully complied.

Many deaf people to this day still ask how it was possible for me to be raised this way. They wonder why my own mother and father (who, because of their own deafness, probably understood my plight better than anyone else) didn't tell everyone to back off. If my parents knew from firsthand experience that sign language was my most accessible form of communication, why did they step aside when it was taken away from me?

There were plenty of reasons—many of them with political, educational, and psychological ramifications—but the number one reason was the simple fact that at the time, I just wasn't deaf enough. I could no longer hear like I used to, but I wasn't quite deaf, either. I was in this hard of hearing netherworld that's also known as being "on the fence." My residual hearing and speech at the time were just *so close* to that of a hearing person. Back then, I could still hold a decent phone conversation, even if I sometimes had to ask people to repeat things.

Since I was teetering between two worlds, most people encouraged me to hold on to the world of sound. If I had been born completely deaf, it might have been a totally different story. But I was *so close*. So my grandparents did everything in their power to cling tightly to whatever hearing and speech I had left, and their hope was to find a way to improve upon it.

In this frenzied quest for normal hearing, doctors and so-called experts bombarded us with the old *it's a hearing world* routine. This meant I needed to wear hearing aids and work on my speech at all times. Sign language? Out of the question. The doctors told my family to make sure my deaf parents did not use sign language in my presence. Their logic behind this? They feared signing would destroy my ability to use speech. The experts had spoken, and that was that. As a result my parents would still sign to each other, but at the same time they tried their best to use voice when conversing directly with me. Hence, I grew up to be a very rare oddity in the deaf world: A deaf child of deaf parents who couldn't sign worth a damn until his mid-twenties.

This pathological approach to deafness is the hardest part of the book for me to write about. Not because it was a difficult experience; quite the contrary, it was a learning experience. I share it with some reluctance because I know hindsight is 20/20. I don't want my family kicking

13

themselves in the butt for doing what others told them was the right thing to do. To this day, my grandmother (on the rare occasions we have frank discussions about deafness) has still expressed feelings of remorse over something that was not her fault at all. Besides, how can you blame people for wanting what they truly believe is best for you? My grandmother has at various times remarked, "We were only doing what the doctors told us to do," and she wonders if she made a huge, irreparable mistake. She did not.

While she and my grandfather were encouraging me to grow closer to the hearing world, they were also helping me go through the best educational programs in the state. Educational programs which, by far, blew away anything that any deaf program had to offer at the time. (I'll get back to this topic later.) If you ask me, the trade-off was worth it. I owe my grandparents a ton of thanks. I would not have the literary skills to write this book in the first place without their involvement in my educational endeavors.

Likewise, my parents have at times expressed their own feelings of remorse. Namely, "Hey, we should have said something when the doctors wouldn't let you sign." As their friends still ask them why they didn't speak up for their rights back then, my parents often struggle to come up with an answer that makes sense. Keep in mind, however, that those were the days when there were few TTYs, no relay services, no captioned TV, no universal acceptance of a Deaf culture, and so on. ASL had yet to be recognized as a bona fide language in its own right. Without that kind of power, there really weren't any good opportunities for me in the Deaf world. That would come later, in due time. So for the time being, my parents went along with whatever the hearing world said was best.

3

::

My family background is somewhat unusual compared to the average deaf person. According to most sources, about ninety percent of deaf people have hearing parents. The ten percent of deaf people who have deaf parents are often considered the lucky ones. While a great number of deaf children with hearing parents fall behind in terms of linguistic development because they cannot hear the spoken language of their parents, deaf children of deaf parents experience no such communication gap. Their language, American Sign Language, is visual instead of aural—but a language nonetheless. This crucial access to language allows normal linguistic and cognitive development to take place, with the many learning experiences that arise naturally amongst parents and children who can communicate effectively.

And then there are the social advantages, such as never being left out of conversations and enjoying all kinds of family outings. Deaf children of deaf parents usually have access to everything going on around them. There is no wondering what anyone said, none of the painful *never mind, it wasn't important* brush-offs that are all too common with hearing relatives and friends who don't sign. In deaf families, the information is right there in ASL for deaf children to enjoy and assimilate.

All in all, deaf children of deaf parents are considered lucky because:

- They have a strong linguistic background, including a better grasp of both ASL and English.

- They live in a more sociably favorable home environment.
- They are also held in high esteem by the deaf community in general, and tend to have strong leadership qualities that help them gain power and prestige. The skills they pick up while immersed in the deaf world are often skills that they can carry over and utilize in the hearing world.

So, in my case, *what happened?* My family experience has been anything but what you'd expect from a deaf child of deaf parents. People today still see me signing and assume I'm hearing, hard of hearing, or a "hearing-minded" deaf guy. Often, their jaws drop when they find out I come from a deaf family. And they scratch their heads even more when I try to explain the dynamics of my family background.

No matter what I say, the question always remains: How could a deaf child be surrounded by so much deafness in his family and not internalize it as part of his own identity? It's a good question that takes quite an effort to answer.

To many deaf people, having deaf parents is a badge of honor. I understand why this is so, and of course I'm proud of my folks. But while I was growing up, I never had a clue that this was such a big deal. After all, hearing family members were acting on the doctors' advice to fix—and therefore deny—my deafness. This convinced me that deafness was something to be ashamed of, not proud of.

On top of that, my mother's closest friends in the deaf community also happened to have deaf children. This led me to the erroneous conclusion that it was mostly deaf people who had deaf kids. I always had the impression we were a tiny, secluded, and flawed population. I personally thought we were a freak show. Being admonished for signing only made it worse. It led me to believe we'd be ridiculed in public if we ever openly displayed our deafness. Yes, I was actually ashamed of who I was.

16

In the meantime, I didn't know that there were millions of deaf and hard of hearing people all over the world. I didn't know that a great number of them were proud to be deaf. And I had no idea that most of them would love to have deaf parents as I did. I never really appreciated how lucky I was to have deaf parents who understood my struggles until I was college-age, when deaf friends of mine made a big fuss over it.

And when people try to figure out how a deaf child of deaf parents can go twenty-plus years with minimal use of sign language, they look at my family background for answers—and find even more questions. Further adding to the confusion is the fact that I have plenty of other deaf relatives besides my mother and father. Whereas my mother is the only deaf person on her side of the family, my father's side is predominantly deaf.

My father's late parents, Cloyd Drolsbaugh and Marjorie (Margie) Schooley Drolsbaugh were deaf. Cloyd came from a hearing family, but Margie's family has a long history of deafness. There are several deaf aunts, uncles, and cousins from the Schooley family whom I've been in touch with from time to time. In fact, there was sort of an odd family reunion when I later attended Gallaudet University. My two distant cousins, Trina Schooley and Dan Warthling, were also enrolled at Gallaudet, and none of us really knew each other until then. Imagine bumping into two people in a big university, getting a good conversation going, and then realizing, *hey, we're family.* Weird, yes, but it gives you an idea of how large my father's family is.

And while my mother's hearing family was close-knit and living in Philadelphia, my father's was spread out all over Pennsylvania. Many are in Scranton/Wilkes-Barre and Juniata County, most of whom I have yet to meet. My paternal grandparents, Margie and Cloyd, had lived in Philadelphia for a considerable time, but had moved back to Scranton when I was six or seven years old. Margie would again relocate to Philadelphia when I was about

17

thirteen. By then, Cloyd had died and Margie wound up marrying Michael Novak (also deaf).

It must be noted that my contact with the deaf side of the family, due to geographic factors, ranged from occasional to sporadic. We usually got together during Christmas, Easter, or someone's birthday. The deaf family members I saw most frequently were my grandmother Margie (who we affectionately called Nana), my step-grandfather Mike, and my Uncle Bob and Aunt Libby.

There are a variety of reasons why my exposure to deaf family members didn't result in my becoming a native ASL signer. First of all, during the early years of my life, I was hearing or pretty close to hearing. I did not have an urgent need to pick up sign language. I could understand my parents' signing, but I hardly signed much myself. When I did sign, it was mostly basic signs mixed up with "home signs" that were just enough to get the message through.

Also, not all of the deaf people in my family are very fluent in ASL. Most of them have used local and home signs that were not prevalent in mainstream deaf society. A number of them had attended oral schools where sign language was not permitted. So they, too, were late in picking up sign language—and thus they were not native signers.

Some of my relatives were hearing or hard of hearing at an early age before later going deaf, such as my father and Uncle Bob. (I followed this pattern myself.) They often used a combination of signing and voice depending on who they were interacting with. Most of my recollections of family get-togethers evoke memories of a communication style closer to what is known as Sim-Com (simultaneous communication, utilizing both voice and sign). My mother and my Aunt Libby—both prelingually deaf—are the exceptions and have always used ASL, and I do recall other family members signing more fluently while in deaf clubs or other situations where most everyone else was deaf.

18

But as wonderful and unique as my father's deaf family may have been, I only saw them occasionally. It was with my mother's hearing family where I spent a much greater amount of time. And when my hearing loss was first discovered, they were absolutely devastated. (By contrast, my father's family just shrugged and life went on. It was no big deal to them.) As previously mentioned, my mother's family searched for professional advice that turned out to be anything but. They wound up following doctors' orders and discouraged me from signing. Somehow, they got my parents to go along with this. The message was clear to me and I internalized it: Deafness and ASL were bad, bad, bad.

Another explanation for my initially poor signing skills can be found by taking a closer look at my peers: Virtually all of them were hearing. The neighborhood kids I played with were hearing, and so were my classmates at school. When my parents visited Uncle Bob and Aunt Libby I would play with their hearing daughters, Mary and Nora. Anyone who knows anything about sociology will tell you that we learn most from our peers, so perhaps this is yet another reason why I didn't sign that much at an early age. Monkey see, monkey do. All of my peers were using voice so I did the same. Since I was postlingually deaf and still had enough residual hearing to be able to talk, I did. To me, being surrounded by hearing peers meant I had to be like them. I managed to do reasonably well most of the time. Later on, I would inevitably stumble.

Although I was often on the hearing side of the fence, it's not like I was completely shut off from the deaf world. How could I be? After all, I was born into it. No matter how much pressure there was to adapt to the hearing world, my parents were still a part of Deaf Culture. Besides my deaf family, I got to see other deaf people when my parents took me with them to the local deaf club. I saw many deaf adults, but perhaps I was not deaf enough myself to relate to them. I did, however, get a good taste of what the deaf world was like.

Back in those days, TTYs had just gone on the market. They were noisy, oversized machines that were no substitute for face-to-face conversations. Many deaf people had yet to get a TTY around the time I was a kid so they often went to the local deaf club on a weekly or monthly basis. This resulted in a phenomenon that I call the infamous Deaf Chat Syndrome. It was not uncommon to stay until the wee hours of the morning as each gathering was an opportunity to catch up on a month's worth of news. Likewise, when deaf friends visited each other, the visits were often unannounced and would last for hours.

My mother would take me on such visits. Usually we visited her good friend Carol. Often, I would watch my mother in amazement: *Doesn't she ever run out of things to say?* Apparently not! Although I enjoyed playing with Carol's children, by ten p.m. I'd had enough. And then the whining would start:

Can we go home now?

My mother would say, "Yes, in just a few more minutes." Those minutes would turn into hours, and my whining would grow louder.

I wanna go home, now!

At this juncture my mother would tell me to get my jacket—we were just about out of there. So I'd put on my jacket, my mother would finally head for the door, and... chat some more. I'd tug at her pants as she stood in the hallway chatting up a storm.

For the umpteenth time, I would remind her it was time to go home. Finally, she would move to the doorway. The doorway where she stopped in her tracks and continued yakking. It seemed that each conversational tidbit took on a life of its own. Heaven forbid somebody briefly mentioned something new on the way out, for a brand new conversation would be spawned right on the spot. For example:

"Okay, I'll see you next week... don't forget to tell Laura I said hello."

"Oh, sure, I saw Laura last week. She's going to the shore with Ted."

"What? She's seeing Ted now? Last time I saw her... blah, blah, blah." Blah, blah, blah, ad infinitum, ad nauseum. Yes, it was annoying. But I didn't realize this was the deaf way of catching up on conversation that couldn't happen anywhere else. Hearing people chat with each other all the time at work, in line at the grocery store, and so on. It doesn't work that way with deaf people (although in today's modern era, emails and text messaging—not to mention videophones—have soothed our pent-up need to get out and talk to somebody). So when a group of deaf friends get together, you know they're going to yak for hours on end.

All I can say about this experience is that I learned how to become a very patient kid, and that no conversation was over until my mother actually started the car and backed out of the driveway. I just chalked it up as something that went on in my mother's deaf world. For as much as I made fun of her for her unlimited chat potential, I would eventually discover that it was hereditary. Years later, I would succumb to Deaf Chat Syndrome myself. I even wrote an article about it, ingeniously titled *Help! I'm Signing and I Can't Shut Up!* Maybe as an eight year old, I never knew it—but perhaps I was subconsciously taking notes and learning how to be culturally Deaf. I was always fascinated with my parent's deaf friends, the deaf clubs they went to, and their wholesome sense of humor. But as a youngster, somehow I was still on the outside looking in.

4

∷

Once I began second grade at Houston School, it became more and more obvious that I wouldn't survive there. My class was considerably larger—about twenty or twenty-five children. There was more information to learn, information that simply went over my head. I remember taking spelling tests where the teacher would walk around the room reciting the words we needed to write down, and I routinely handed in a blank piece of paper. I felt terribly inadequate when I did so. There was no way at this age that I could reason that it was not my fault. Based on the actions of hearing family members, teachers, and students, I perceived that I was some kind of defective freak. Deafness was bad, I was bad. I needed to be fixed.

Being "fixed" was no walk in the park. My family kept sending me to doctors and audiologists, all the while reinforcing my mistaken belief that I was a freak of nature. My ears were tested so often that I learned by rote the entire word sheet the audiologists would read at varying frequencies:

"Say the word... *hot dog.*"

"Say the word... *toothbrush.*" This was worse than Chinese water torture. Say the word... *nauseated.*

Despite the way I felt in the audiologist booth, however, it is not my intention to attack the audiology profession. Audiologists are crucial for the purpose of assessment and placement. There is, however, a reasonable limit to how many times you can be tested and retested. My limit was exceeded to the point where even the ENT specialist told my grandfather to get a grip and to start accepting my hearing loss.

Furthermore, it didn't do me any good at all to be placed in an environment where I would repeatedly fail. There is no actual pass or fail as far as audiological tests are concerned—it's just an assessment, not a quiz—but no one took the time to explain that to me. They should have.

Today, an increasing number of audiologists know sign language. They are able to explain to deaf children that hearing tests are merely evaluations which will help other people understand how to accommodate their needs. In my opinion, this ability to communicate with clients should be an absolute must. I say this because I felt like an insignificant guinea pig when I was tested. I was completely terrorized; I felt like I was failing miserably, and I also felt like I was letting my family down.

Most of the time, I didn't mind the "raise your hand at the beep" routine because it was relatively simple. If I heard a beep, I would raise my hand; if I didn't hear a beep, I didn't know I missed anything. But when it came to the part where I had to repeat words and sentences the audiologist said—without being permitted to read her lips—that's when I felt like an incompetent fool.

Incompetent fool or not, I was fitted with two hearing aids which did nothing but make my life even more miserable. Hearing adults suddenly expected me to hear everything that was said, further intimidating me into believing I had to be like them. I began *nodding*, saying "yes" to everything people said without having the slightest clue as to what they were talking about (that's right—I was a walking bobblehead doll).

Yes, other people's voices were certainly louder when I wore the hearing aids, but my ability to understand their speech showed no significant improvement. The only advantage of having hearing aids, for me, was that I could actually hear the toilet flush from the next room. This must have been culturally significant because it was around that time that the first toilet was flushed on national television, when Archie Bunker did the honors on *All in the Family*. I am eternally grateful to my family and medical professionals for making it possible for me to share this special moment.

In school though, there was nothing special about wearing hearing aids. I was made fun of and ridiculed. Second grade was the only time in my life where I routinely got into fights and received report cards that said my behavior left much to be desired. It was obvious that there was no way I could keep this up.

At this juncture, my grandparents went out and did the best favor they ever could have done for me at the time. They did their homework, checked out a number of possibilities, and enrolled me at Plymouth Meeting Friends School. A small private school outside of Philadelphia, PMFS offered a cozy learning environment that would be a welcome change from the crowded classes at Houston School. Also, I didn't know it while I was there, but PMFS' Quaker background and philosophy would later have a tremendous impact on my personal growth.

Upon entering the third grade at PMFS, I was, of course, apprehensive. I assumed I would be the laughingstock of the class and initially kept my guard up at all times. Fortunately, my assumption was wrong. With PMFS' small student population there were only about eight kids in each class. Not only that, but each class also had a teacher's aide, meaning the student-teacher ratio was a comfortable 4:1. It was very clear from the start that I would get some much-needed individual attention. It helped immensely. Anytime I misunderstood instructions (and that was quite often), the teacher's aide would zoom to the rescue, fill me in on the details, and I would be right up with the rest of the class in schoolwork.

While it was clear from the start that I would be in good hands academically, I was still concerned about my social life. Memories of the taunts and fights I had put up with at Houston School were still fresh in my mind. However, my third grade teacher, Mrs. Paul, had gone out of her way to make me feel welcome at PMFS. She

24

had previously explained to her class that there would be a hard of hearing boy joining them, and she encouraged them to ask questions so that they knew what to expect. She encouraged them to speak clearly so that I could read their lips and feel like I was a part of the class. I was certainly grateful when I noticed that I was accepted warmly. There was some curiosity about what I was like and how my hearing aids worked, but no one made fun of me. Mrs. Paul did an excellent job of helping us all go through this transition.

Old habits die hard though, so I was still on my guard for a while before I completely settled down at PMFS. I figured it was only a matter of time before some moron would poke fun at me and I'd have to defend myself. Most of the kids quickly got along with me, but I was just waiting for that one idiot who always has to screw everything up. And there was indeed one particular boy, Quinn, who seemed to be making fun of me. Actually, he was making fun of everyone and everything. He was one of those fun-loving types who was always laughing and cracking jokes. Nonetheless, I eyed him suspiciously and didn't like him. Anytime he laughed, I figured that it had to be something about me.

Finally, on one cold winter day, we were all outside playing snow football. We were having a blast tackling each other in the snow and sliding all over the place. Suddenly, when I had the ball, Quinn delivered a good hit and knocked the wind out of me. Normally I would have been a good sport but this particular hit knocked a hearing aid right off my ear. It was a quick and sudden reminder to everyone that I was *different*.

To make matters worse, the battery had come loose and fallen out. It was lost somewhere on a vast field, hidden under six inches of snow. I made a fuss over the battery but actually it was just my pride that was hurt. When we returned to class, Mrs. Paul heard about what had happened from one of the students. She approached me and asked about the battery. A number of students were standing around her, showing as much concern as my teacher.

"Do you have another battery at home?" asked Mrs. Paul.

"Nope", I said, feeling sorry for myself. Quinn, the guy who I knew would make fun of me, walked up.

"How much does it cost for a new one?"

"About one hundred dollars," I whined.

One hundred dollars, my ass. You can replace a hearing aid battery as quickly and as cheaply as a regular wristwatch battery. But I was the class freak (or so I thought), so I figured if the equipment I had was incredibly expensive, then it must be incredibly *important*. Right after I gave this incredibly exaggerated value of the hearing aid battery, some of the students volunteered to go out and look for it.

And look for it they did, on a football field covered with six inches of snow. Given that a hearing aid battery is less than half the size of a marble, this would be much harder than looking for the proverbial needle in a haystack. It should have been touching enough that they were so considerate that they tried looking for it. But they went way beyond that. They searched high and low and *found it*. They actually found the damn thing. It was none other than Quinn who rushed in, smiling proudly, and handed me my one hundred dollar battery. The lesson I learned in friendship that day was worth a million bucks.

After the hearing aid incident, I became more comfortable at PMFS and had no problem getting along with others. I related quite well with my classmates who were as accommodating as the staff. My best friend, Norman, would call me up on the phone during evenings and weekends, patiently repeating words or even spelling them until I understood what he was saying. In class, other students often took the burden off of the teacher aide by repeating instructions or assignments that I didn't understand. With this kind of support I no longer felt ashamed or embarrassed by my deafness.

I began to feel I fit in so well that I was practically as hearing as everyone else. When it was suggested that I take up speech therapy, I gladly consented because I viewed it as something that would make me even more hearing. (It would, my grandparents assured me, help me speak the same way as everyone else.) So I figured, *Why not?* I was so encouraged by the way I was fitting in at PMFS that I perceived speech therapy as icing on the cake. I was finally going to look, act, and speak like a hearing person.

My speech teacher, Mrs. Wells, was a funny, highly creative person who knew how to turn a dreary activity into something a whole lot more fun. She did not exhibit the *we need to fix you* sense of urgency that I had perceived from other professionals. If I pronounced a word wrong she would make a funny face, get me laughing, and encourage me to get it right. When I did get a tough word right, I would gleefully repeat it until she screamed, "Aaarrggghh!!! No more! I'm sick of that word!" The more success I had, the more she let me drive her up the wall. I would come home and brag to my family that I was so good at what I did that I was driving my speech teacher nuts. I was on the road to Hearing Person, and very proud of it.

After about two years of speech therapy, however, I had a rather humbling wake-up call. My mother had introduced me to a hearing acquaintance of hers, with whom I proudly held a brief conversation. Although my mother's friend knew sign language, I kept my hands to myself and used my speech. I managed to go through the customary "How are you?" and "Nice to meet you," all without having to ask this woman to repeat anything she said. On top of that, I didn't even stutter once, smoothly going through those damned Rs that used to give me a hard time. I was very proud of myself and beamed accordingly.

27

My pride, however, soon took a nosedive. As my mother's friend walked to her car, I caught her signed conversation with my mom:

"Is your son hard of hearing?"

"Yes," my mom responded, "His hearing is slowly going down—just like his father and Uncle Bob. It's hereditary."

"Yes, I could tell by his voice . . ."

My heart sank. I would continue to do my best to be as hearing as possible for the next several years, but this was a real smack in the face. Reality was a bummer. People would continue pushing for me to be as hearing as possible, and I would still do my best to comply. Deep down, however, I knew I would always be different.

Fortunately, if there was ever a good place to be different and still be accepted anyway, PMFS was it. As for all of the issues relating to deafness which I am bringing up in this book, there is nothing further to say regarding my years at PMFS. I was part of one big family, and I loved every minute of it. I don't recall sticking out like a sore thumb; in fact, grades three through six were the wonder years for me. It must have been the calm before the storm. We'll get to that storm later... the adolescent hell also known as high school.

5

∶ ∶

School was not the only place where I would struggle with deafness. There were other aspects of life to deal with, such as religion. My experience with religion has been just as complicated as anything I went through in school, perhaps even more so. School is where we learn our ABCs and the basics of life with all of our peers; religion is more of an internal struggle, a path we ultimately choose to pursue alone.

My path towards spiritual growth has taken countless detours, but every venture off the beaten path has been a blessing in disguise. For the most part my search for the meaning of life has taken me through Judaism, Christianity, Quakerism, and a deep fascination with Eastern Philosophy. I've never really fit into one particular traditional religion, though. Some may argue that this is a negative consequence of deafness, but I choose to look at it differently. The positive side to all of this is that by never actually fitting into just one, I could appreciate them all. It took a long time and a lot of soul-searching, but eventually I would find my own personal niche.

The first step, for me, was Judaism. Although my mother and father did not always observe religious holidays at home, my mother came from a Jewish family that played by all the rules. In fact, my grandfather himself was an ordained rabbi. A pretty good one, I must add. My character has been greatly shaped by the lessons I learned through him. Although my hearing loss prevented me from completely assimilating the religion he loved so much, I was still greatly influenced. I might have had all of the rules of organized religion fly over my head—but at least I managed to pick up the *essence* of them.

For example, one day I was riding on the highway with my grandfather; all of a sudden, some moron zoomed up a ramp, ignored a yield sign, and cut us off. All my grandfather did was apply the brakes, let the maniac cut through, and then go about his driving as if nothing had happened.

"Grandpop?" I asked. "Why did you let him do that?" Grandpop just smiled.

"I don't want to prove, with a broken arm, that I had the right of way."

That lesson in humility and egolessness stuck with me for a long time. In this day and age of people flipping each other the finger and shooting semi-automatic weapons on the highways, we could sure use more people like good-old Grandpop.

For the most part, my involvement with religion was essentially to learn by doing, and to absorb anecdotal lessons like the highway incident with my grandfather. I never really learned any specific religious dogma or the meaning behind it. I never fully understood why my grandparents would light a candle at certain times on certain days. But as they went about their daily lives in accordance with their religious philosophy, I was able to emulate general behaviors such as being compassionate and caring about each other. Like I said, I pretty much skipped the dogma and went straight to the essence.

Other than that, I generally enjoyed accompanying my grandmother and grandfather to the synagogue, even if I never really understood what was going on. I enjoyed the half-hour drive, playing brainteaser games with Grandmom the whole way ("I'm thinking of a number between one and one hundred"), and then proudly watching Grandpop preach his stuff at the synagogue. My impression was somewhere along the lines of *Yessiree, that's my grandfather up there. What the hell he's saying, I have no idea, but that's my grandfather up there.* Regardless of how much I understood, I was proud of him.

As I got older though, I began having problems with religion. The first problem, simply put, was that everyone inevitably expected me to understand what was going on. While religion to my mother and father simply meant showing up at whatever family events were going on, my grandparents took a more vested interest in my religious development. When I was about ten or eleven, I had made so much progress as a student at Plymouth Meeting Friends School that they expected me to likewise learn quickly in the synagogue. I was briefly enrolled in a Sunday Hebrew School, but this completely bombed. It was like Houston School all over again. I had no idea what people were talking about, there were too many kids, and I was being made fun of. There was no way I could learn Hebrew in there. I had enough trouble understanding people speaking plain English, so what did they expect?

Did I ever speak up? Of course not. Due to the earlier reactions to my deafness by hearing relatives and various professionals, it was already ingrained in my mind that deafness was bad. In a way, I was behaviorally conditioned (in fact, when I took a course on Gestalt Theory and Practice several years later, I learned that this was referred to as being programmed by an *introject*). Anytime I was able to understand hearing people or speak clearly, I was praised; anytime I had difficulty understanding others, or if I mispronounced words, the hearing people in my life would react with grave concern. Deafness was bad, period, so there was no way I could defend myself. I never even looked at it as being treated unfairly because I was deaf; I figured that if I couldn't understand all those people in Hebrew School, it must be my fault.

To make matters even worse, Hebrew School wasn't the half of it. I bombed so badly that my grandfather mercifully bailed me out and decided he would teach me himself. He was determined that by age thirteen, I would

31

know enough to have a Bar Mitzvah. (To his delight, I eventually did.) And so he began to teach me. He did quite well, but it was not always a smooth ride.

Yes, Grandpop was very patient and accommodating as he taught me what I needed to know. What I got from him in these individual sessions, I had no problem assimilating. Everything else, such as whatever went on in the synagogue or during family celebrations went over my head as always. No one really understood this except for my own parents, who weren't really involved anyway. For whatever reason, be it denial or just plain ignorance, everyone else in the family had unrealistic expectations. As far as they were concerned I was a hearing, Jewish boy. A common scenario: A day or so before any significant Jewish holiday, a hearing family member would smile at me and say, "Mark, do you know what tomorrow is?" I would instinctively cringe, for I knew it was all downhill after this.

"Uhhhhh," I'd stammer meekly.

"Oh, come on, you know what it is! Tomorrow is Purim. Do you know what Purim is all about?" I was completely cornered in situations like this. At best, I would take a wild guess. Most of the time, I would shrug helplessly. This would be enough to set off the disaster I knew was coming. First, it would be a gasp of shock, followed by heads shaking disapprovingly. Then came the barrage:

"Mark! You should know what it is! It's your heritage! You should know!"

Yeah, right. I should know. For the life of me, I wish I could turn back the clock and shoot back:

How the hell should I know? You guys chatter incessantly and expect me to just soak it up like a sponge? Hasn't anyone told you I'm deaf? If it's so damn important, why don't you learn sign language and then tell me what it is I need to know? You should know what it's like to be deaf. Don't be giving me any of this "you should know" . . .

Of course, I never spoke up. *Deafness is bad. Be hearing. Good boy, be hearing.*

32

Obviously, my hearing family could frustrate me sometimes. Yet if they gave me a hard time about my deafness, they had no idea they were doing so. At least in other ways they gave me plenty of love and attention. So if I had any bad experiences with my family, they were always related to deafness or religion. Those are just two aspects of my world. In many other aspects, my family was loving and supportive. We all play a number of roles in life; some of mine, for example, are son, grandson, husband, father, student, athlete, and deaf person. Most of my roles have been supported one hundred percent by my family. For my role as deaf person, they just weren't sure what to do. And neither was I, seeing how I meekly tiptoed around the subject whenever it arose.

Despite my early frustrations with Judaism, it needs to be mentioned that nonetheless, somehow I was greatly influenced by Jewish philosophy. My grandfather's wisdom and my grandmother's strong family values are parts of my background that I will always hold on to. It gave me a foundation from which I could build on. There would be more religions that I would become involved in, all of them shaping in some way my philosophy of life, but I will never forget where I came from.

School and religion, no doubt, were rollercoaster rides featuring both joy and despair. While we all go through the normal growing pains in our own unique ways, we also need some sort of outlet to make life more bearable for us. For me, this outlet was baseball. Away from the pressures of school, and away from the high expectations of my family, I just threw myself into baseball full-time each summer.

I was fortunate to grow up in a time when my role models, the Philadelphia Phillies of the '70s and '80s, consistently played together as a team. This was long before the combination of free agency and out-of-control salaries created a lot of player movement. I felt connected to the Phillies during my childhood because I could count

33

on my favorite players returning the following year. It was like Steve Carlton, Mike Schmidt, Larry Bowa, Garry Maddox, and several others were always there. Nowadays it's not so simple. I'm just glad that as a kid, I got to see the same guys bust their butts each year with a true love for the game. I looked up to them and always wanted to emulate them.

And emulate them I did, playing baseball from twelve noon until whenever the sun went down. In my neighborhood this meant whiffle ball, stickball, sandlot hardball, and eventually organized Little League. Looking back, I realize that during those sandlot days, I was immortal. I was too young to be aware of all of the hard struggles that would be waiting for me a few years later. I was too young to understand that someday we all grow old and eventually kick the bucket. I was just too young to worry about it. This must be what all the great masters have meant when they preached the virtues of *living in the now.* By playing ball all day, oblivious to all the hassles of the adult world, we had a taste of nirvana. It's sad that in today's era many kids are exposed too soon to the horrors of drugs and violence. They grow up too fast and miss out on the carefree, greatly rewarding childhood experiences that we all deserve. I was lucky to live in a time and place where I could just let go and taste the good life.

My neighborhood was the Mt. Airy section of Philadelphia. It was a melting pot of Irish, Italian, African-American, Jewish, you name it. I wound up becoming close friends with an African-American family on my block even though it seemed as if we didn't have much in common. In this family was a boy my age named Sekou, who became my best friend. Even though we were culturally different, we shared an immense love for baseball. Sekou had no problem with me being deaf; I had no problem with him being black. What was the big deal? We had a lot of fun playing baseball, and that was that.

To other people though, it was a big deal. I didn't realize this for at first because I was blissfully oblivious to the existence of racial tension. But after playing countless hours of baseball in the safe confines of my backyard, my friends and I eventually became real good at it. We would play against other sandlot teams and we routinely beat them. We wanted to expand our horizons but soon learned the unfortunate lesson that other people were not as open-minded as we would have liked.

It really hit me one day when my mom took me for a drive through the suburbs. There was a Little League game being played on an incredibly beautiful grass field, complete with scoreboards and dugouts. I'd never seen anything like it. I got excited and told my mom that it would be perfect for Sekou and me. I knew right away that we could compete at the same level as the kids playing on this immaculate field. But my mom shook her head sadly and began to explain something I could not understand. We were only five or six years removed from the Civil Rights movement and Martin Luther King Jr.'s tragic assassination, and there were still some neighborhoods where blacks were simply not welcome. As my mom pointed out, there was not one single black player on the field I was so enamored with.

While Sekou was legally entitled to play on any Little League team he wanted, there were many in this particular neighborhood who would make his life miserable, my mom explained. I could not make any sense out of all this. Here was one of few people who unconditionally accepted me for who I was, and his *skin color* was a big deal? This was stupid. As far as I was concerned, Little League could wait.

My friends and I continued to play sandlot ball all summer. It was around this time when Sekou's family taught me something that I would not fully grasp until much later. While I was struggling with my deafness—constantly trying to act like a hearing boy and constantly worrying about what other people thought—Sekou's family held their heads up high. They were black, they were proud, and they didn't give a damn that some prejudiced morons in the world couldn't accept them for who they were. They often dressed in beautiful African clothes. Their house was loaded with African paintings, sculptures, and artifacts. Sekou's parents always welcomed me into their house, and they proudly shared their world with me.

One afternoon, Sekou's father took me along with the kids to their favorite barbershop. I was in a room full of about twenty other people, none of them white. I was the only one. I was about ten or eleven at the time and it was a strange feeling, sticking out the way that I did. Sekou's father wanted to give me an idea of what it feels like to be a racial minority, and he succeeded. For the first time, I really understood how Sekou must have felt whenever we ventured into a predominantly white neighborhood for a sandlot game. I realize now that there is no better lesson to learn than to have empathy and compassion for another's perspective, and to be able to walk a mile in someone else's moccasins.

Looking back, I also realize that I could have done a better job of learning another lesson: How to be proud of your own culture. If my parents and I had half the pride in being deaf that Sekou's family had in being black, then most of our problems would have been eliminated right there. Of course, I learned this lesson slowly, given my tendency to do things the hard way.

Eventually, Sekou's family packed their bags and moved downtown so they could live closer to the church they routinely attended. I would make other friends, both black and white, and we all kept playing baseball. But before Sekou moved, there was one game we played that I'll never forget. We were challenged to a game in another part of the neighborhood, in a sandlot field behind Grace Church on Gowen Avenue. The challenge was issued by an all-white baseball team a few blocks away and they told us to make sure we had at least nine players; this

36

was going to be real *baseball,* not a makeshift game where a trash can lid doubled as home plate.

We looked around and found as many neighborhood kids as we could. We managed to round up about twelve people, but only five or six of us were bona fide baseball players. We had to recruit some guys who didn't play that much (if at all), because positions needed to be filled. For a while there we actually contemplated putting my dog in right field. She was good at catching or chasing down balls but didn't have much of an arm.

When we arrived at the sandlot field, we noticed that the other team was *big*. Many of them I had never seen before. My feeling at first was that this was not about baseball, but more likely a black vs. white thing. Someone on the other team made a disparaging remark about me being the only white guy on my team. The first pitch had yet to be thrown, but already racism was rearing its ugly head.

Once the game started though, something wonderful was happening. We all began to have a lot of fun. We forgot about skin color and we focused on baseball. Not that it helped my team though. Our opponents were really good, and they were giving us quite a drubbing. By the ninth inning we were down, 13-0. But we were enjoying ourselves a lot more than the score would have indicated.

With two outs in the top of the ninth, I stepped up to the plate. I ripped a hard line drive down the right-field line and pulled into second base with a double. The next batter was Teddy, one of those fill-in players we had pulled out of nowhere. Whoever he was, he ripped the stuffing out of the next pitch for a solid base hit, bringing me home with our only run of the game. As I crossed the plate, the team mobbed me like we had just won the seventh game of the World Series, screaming and hugging and all that. It was the warmest moment I've ever experienced in all sports, including championships that later I would be a part of in high school and organized baseball. We all learned something about brotherhood that day. Both teams, black and white.

6

::

As the elementary school years drew to a close, it was time to start thinking about high school. During my final year at Plymouth Meeting Friends School (which runs from kindergarten to grade six), my grandparents looked for another school where I would continue to receive a quality education. They'd heard that Germantown Friends School was one of the best schools in Philadelphia and decided that this would be my next step. Since GFS is also a Friends' school, it would provide a continuation of the teaching style and Quaker philosophy I had grown accustomed to at PMFS. A wonderful program with a rigorous academic curriculum, this was practically Harvard High School. Virtually all GFS graduates go on to greater academic achievement in post secondary programs—including a considerable number of Ivy League colleges—a phenomenal success rate that continues to this day.

Along with five other PMFS classmates, I took an entrance exam at GFS that was supposed to determine whether or not we had what it takes to survive the challenging curriculum. A few weeks later, we whooped it up in celebration when we found out we'd all been accepted.

Oops, not so fast. The other five were definitely in. As far as the entrance exam indicated, so was I—but a few things needed to be cleared up first. The faculty at GFS had heard about my promising academic potential, but they'd also heard about my deafness. This was not the cute, cozy environment of PMFS; this was a relatively large school with nine hundred students. It needed to be assessed as to whether or not I could survive in what would prove to be a difficult environment for a deaf kid. A one-day visit was scheduled so that I could get a taste of life at GFS.

This one-day visit is granted to all incoming GFS students so that they know what to expect when they enroll. For me, however, this visit was going to be the final say in whether or not I would be accepted. Not only would I get to see what life at GFS was like, but also the faculty would be evaluating my ability to function in a large, hearing school.

When I arrived at GFS for my introductory visit, I knew very well what the stakes were. My grandfather had explained, loud and clear, the real purpose of this visit. I knew he was really rooting for me to get in and I didn't want to let him down.

To GFS' credit, they didn't beat around the bush. I was escorted to a Mr. Emerson's office, and he got right down to the bottom line: He was happy to see me there, but he also wanted to see how my deafness would affect me in the classroom. I would attend a number of classes and then return at the end of the day to discuss how it went. My escort for the day was then ushered in. I smiled in delight—it was Ian, an old neighborhood friend of mine whom I knew very well. Whether this was prearranged or just plain dumb luck, I don't know. Either way, I was certainly grateful to have him showing me around. Of course we hit it off well, because we'd grown up next door from each other. This was a considerable advantage because I was at ease when interacting with him. Ian also took the time to tactfully explain to his friends that I was deaf, and they treated me with kindness and respect. For a day, it looked like this deaf stranger had waltzed in and quickly won over his potential classmates. The teachers noticed this and must have thought, *Hey, this deaf kid is pretty cool. He can hang with the best of them.*

To be honest though, ninety-five percent of the time I had no idea what was going on. It was a big school and I found it rather intimidating. If it weren't for Ian and his circle of friends, I probably would have run out of there completely terrorized. Classes were a blur; I didn't understand one word the teachers and students said. I just smiled when other people smiled, chuckled when other people chuckled, and tried my best to look like I fit in. I didn't want to let my grandfather down, and I didn't plan to. I was getting into this school even if I had to put on an Oscar performance to do it.

Finally, at the end of the day, I returned to Mr. Emerson's office. Conversing with him was no problem because I was pretty much okay at one-to-one conversations. It was the groups—especially classroom discussion—that had me lost in space.

Mr. Emerson opened our meeting by asking how my day had gone. I replied that it had gone just fine. He probed a bit more and asked if my deafness affected my ability to participate in class. I assured him that I was on top of everything. My lip-reading skills, I insisted, allowed me to understand most of what was going on. Yes, I assured him, I had most definitely enjoyed my visit. Then I gave him the same baloney my grandfather told him and everyone else: With a hearing aid, I'm practically the same as any other normal kid. That was it; I was in. I was a bullshitter, but I was in. *The nominee for best actor is, . . .*

Settling in at GFS was not going to be easy. I knew it, and my family knew it. But my grandfather had an encounter with someone who inspired him to give me a little pep talk. He'd bumped into Dr. Cash, a very successful deaf man who happened to be a prominent surgeon. I'd heard of him before and I was surprised to find out that he'd had a long heart-to-heart talk with my grandfather. It was the first time Grandpop had met such a well-to-do deaf adult and he took advantage of the opportunity to discuss a number of issues related to deafness.

Shortly before I began the seventh grade at GFS, my grandfather decided to disclose the entire content of his discussion with Dr. Cash. He looked dead serious.

"Mark, do you remember Dr. Cash, the surgeon? He has a hearing problem just like yours, and he's a doctor. Well, I was talking to him about you going to GFS. He said he doesn't think you're going to make it."

Oh great, I thought, *Nice way to boost my confidence.*

"Incidentally," my grandfather continued, "Dr. Cash himself went to GFS for a short time. It didn't work out. He said that no deaf person ever has, nor ever will graduate from GFS. I think you can prove him wrong."

Now I was getting psyched, and a sense of pride clicked inside me. Yes, I knew Dr. Cash was only being realistic; he knew firsthand that GFS was a tough school for anyone. The school had enough academic challenges as it was—throw in a progressively worsening hearing loss, and that might have been one challenge too many. Nonetheless, I was determined to show that I had what it takes. I knew it was going to be a formidable task, but I was going to make it.

As determined as I was to succeed at GFS, it immediately became a difficult transition. At PMFS everyone had known me, and I had also been one of the best athletes in the whole school. At GFS I was just a face in the crowd, and I was a mediocre athlete among the many students. I was lost in the classroom and relegated to the "B" squad on the soccer team. Yes, these are normal frustrations experienced by anyone who moves to a bigger school. But for me they were magnified—my deafness made it much harder to adapt. It was hard to make new friends, and it was hard to believe I'd ever be comfortable there because I understood so little of what went on. It was a chore trying to read everyone's lips; it was frustrating when homeroom teachers reminded me to wear my hearing aids and sit up front, as if it would help. (It didn't.) Each class was fraught with a considerable amount of stress. I would worry that the teacher would call on me and that I'd make a fool out of

41

myself. Often, I did—it's hard to answer questions you don't understand.

I felt a considerable amount of pressure to fit in with the hearing students. I tried my best to look like I knew what was going on at all times. My daily routine consisted of trying my damnedest to understand what went on in class, yet at the same time maintain an air of nonchalance so that I didn't stick out like a sore thumb. Nonetheless, a teacher would often approach me at the end of class to make sure I was okay. I would quickly brush off the teacher with false assurances that all was fine and dandy. A common scenario:

"Yes, Ms. Wilson, I'm doing fine, no problem."

(A brief pause as the teacher leaves the classroom.)

"Hey, Brian! What did she say the homework was?"

The essence of my seventh and eighth-grade education was to bluff my way through class, then run up to a friendly student I knew I could depend on. I'd check with him to make sure I understood the homework assignment. Then, with that information, I would go home or to the library where I could review and catch up on everything I had missed in class. It wouldn't be too far off base to say that in my early years at GFS, I was self-educated.

Fortunately, I did have a considerable amount of support from certain caring individuals, including some very empathetic classmates. One of them, Dean, was in my Latin class. We played in the same summer baseball league and he knew me well enough to know that I was bluffing my way through Latin.

Often, there were times when I just couldn't understand what the teacher asked me, and my face would turn red with embarrassment and frustration. Rather than risk further ridicule, I would be content with saying, "I don't know," and letting someone else answer the question. Dean was on to me and tried his best to help. Sometimes I would respond with an "I don't know" to a ridiculously easy question and Dean wouldn't let me get away with it. Imagine, for example, a substitute teacher coming in and asking me what my name was.

"Duh, I don't know."

Dean would jump in and help me save face. He would tap me on the shoulder, smile, and repeat the question slowly for me. His mannerisms made it clear that it was okay if I didn't understand what was going on; few people gave me this type of reinforcement, and it was much appreciated.

As for the faculty, they were demanding, but they also genuinely cared. They would challenge us in the classroom, making us think until our brains burst out of our ears. I knew I was in a really good school because the teachers were never satisfied with concrete answers. If you answered correctly on an exam to a question related to *what* had happened, of course you would get credit for it—but there would be red ink comments everywhere on the paper. The teachers also wanted to know *why* it had happened, what the dynamics were, and how things might have been different if . . . You get the idea. This was a school where you learned how to think outside the box. The teachers were not content with just answers; they wanted more questions.

The teachers also took the time for private conferences with their students (incidentally, I had plenty) to make sure we were doing okay and if anything could further be done to facilitate our progress. So if I give the impression at times that I was unhappy at GFS, it had nothing to do with their program; I believe in my heart that GFS is the best high school anywhere. It's just that as the only deaf student, I was often like a fish out of water.

By the end of my first year at GFS, I would be rescued from academic hell by my beloved sport, baseball. Thanks to baseball the year ended on a very positive note. I was a key part of the seventh grade baseball team, and I was finally having fun again. I may have stunk up the soccer field and the basketball court—making only the "B" teams on both—but with baseball it was my turn to shine. We had a great team and I made some more friends. Playing ball is a universal language for kids, so being deaf didn't really matter.

It was around this time that there was a significant change at home. A chance encounter led to my mother accepting a new job at none other than the Pennsylvania School for the Deaf. She worked part-time on some evenings as a dorm counselor, and this was a huge paradigm shift not just for her, but also for me. Occasionally, there were times when my mom took me along with her when she worked a shift at the PSD dorm. It was unbelievable. It was a totally, totally different world.

I have no idea how I can adequately describe what it felt like the first time I walked into a whole school full of deaf children. It was an awakening, a rebirth of sorts, and all communication shackles broke free. I can only attempt to describe how I felt. Mere words can't express it adequately enough, but they will have to do:

Imagine that you were born in some small Atlantis at the bottom of the sea, and the only life you knew was to live in some glass bubble underwater. You could watch all the fish swim and play, but you weren't really a participant in that life; you were nothing more than an observer to most of the things that happened around you. But with the help of technology you could put on scuba gear and swim with the fish. Unfortunately, the gear was heavy and uncomfortable, and as much as it helped you interact with the fish, you never were able to swim like them. You were different and you knew it.

Suddenly, one day, you decided to keep swimming upwards. Your friends, the fish, advised against it.

"Silly boy," they said, "everyone knows it's a liquid world. You have nothing to gain by going up to the surface. Air is too thin, land is too hard. It's a liquid world."

You've heard this argument before, and you've always listened to it. On this occasion, however, you felt that *it was time*. Time to find out who you really were, and everything you were all about. You swam all the way to the surface, and wonder of wonders, you found that there were thousands of people like you! You swam to the shore, and once you set your foot on land you realized you didn't need all of that heavy scuba apparatus. You could run with the legs you were born with, and you could freely breathe in the natural air you were meant to breathe in. You could hold effortless conversations, and have deep, meaningful relationships with others. Freedom at last!

I can just see one of my old hearing classmates reading the above analogy and saying, "So what am I, a flounder?" No offense to my old classmates, but I genuinely felt a sense of freedom and involvement at PSD that I had never experienced anywhere else. When I met the other students in the PSD dorm for the first time, I felt a lightness, a jubilation that had never existed before. No straining to read lips; no struggling to keep up with conversations going on between two or more people; no pressure to pass myself off as a hearing person. We were equals, and I was learning the value of true, meaningful interaction.

Everywhere I went, I could understand clearly what was being said, since everyone at PSD was signing. Although I had been discouraged from signing in my earlier years, I had picked up enough at home while watching my mom and dad sign to each other. Even though I wasn't a completely fluent signer myself, I knew enough to be able to interact with the deaf students at PSD. We played games, watched captioned movies, and had all kinds of fun. I never had to worry about fitting in, or about catching up on missed information. The burden of trying to be something I'm not was temporarily lifted. Sign language made my life bearable again.

Even my grandparents, who had originally cooperated with doctors' advice that I should not sign—on the erroneous premise that it was bad for my speech—took note that it was not the horrendous evil that it was made out to be. When my mother became more involved in the Deaf community through PSD, the changes in her self-esteem and demeanor were so positive that for a short time my grandparents actually enrolled in sign language classes themselves.

One evening in the spring of 1978, PSD held a Springfest event complete with carnival rides, games, fireworks, and a concert featuring songs performed in sign language. It was the most fun I'd ever had in my neighborhood. Deaf and hearing people alike interacted freely amongst each other and had the greatest time. For once, deafness was not bad; it actually seemed cool. My mind was made up then and there: Soon, I would confront my parents.

When school was out and I felt the time was right, I approached my mom one evening and asked if I could transfer to PSD. It wasn't fair for me to be so isolated at GFS; it was no fun being the only deaf student. Except for the spring, when I had baseball games to look forward to, I never really enjoyed going to school in the morning. I dreaded classroom discussion, I dreaded embarrassing myself when I misunderstood the teachers' questions or assignments, and heck, I was always bombing with the girls. While some girls were nice enough to make polite conversation, none of them were able to get to know me on a deeper level. It just didn't click. It was only a communication barrier—not a reflection of who I was—but nonetheless I let this shoot my self-esteem to hell. I assumed that the girls simply wanted to hang out with the cool kids, not disabled geeks like me.

At PSD on the other hand, girls clearly *liked* me. They talked to me freely about anything, and I even had a brief puppy-love thing going with a nice girl there when I was fourteen. Meanwhile, at GFS, I just wasn't getting any action. For a young, horny teenager, that's plenty of reason to transfer out of a school.

Unfortunately, this horny teenager would have to wait. My mother and father gave me an emphatic *no*. I was not going to transfer to PSD. My mother actually gave it some thought and looked into it, and she made a grim discovery that she wasn't sure how to explain.

The fact was, going into the eighth grade at GFS, I had already academically surpassed virtually all of the PSD seniors. In English, math, science, you name it, I'd already done it. At PSD, I would have been taking an academic step backwards. At GFS, there were more mountains to climb. As my mother explained this, tears welled in my eyes.

"But mom, they're my *friends*." My mother could only shake her head sadly. When my father heard how I felt about the whole thing, he tried to console me by sharing his own experience. When he was younger, he had similar academic potential, but he'd had no choice but to attend a deaf school. It did nothing for him. He began to explain a complicated social/academic phenomenon I would not really understand until much later.

Since my father came from a deaf family in Scranton, Pennsylvania, he was able to grow up in an environment where he had access to communication. Developmentally, he was on par with other hearing children. The only difference between deaf children of deaf families and hearing children of hearing families is the mode of communication; in one they sign; in the other they speak.

As many parents will attest, a favorite word of all young toddlers is "Why". Why does it get dark at night, why do I have to take a bath, why is the goldfish floating upside down, why do Aunt Emma's teeth fall out, why am I deaf? Why, why, why?

Whether amusing or annoying, we owe it to our children to answer as many of their whys as possible. When we take the time to do this, children internalize crucial information. This greatly enhances their overall development in terms of thought processing and general knowledge acquisition.

Unfortunately, such favorable environments of communication do not exist for most deaf kids. Ninety percent of deaf children have hearing parents, and usually there's a significant communication gap. Often, hearing parents do not know sign language. The deaf child has to read lips, and reading lips is difficult. Only about thirty-five percent of the spoken language can be lip-read because most sounds are formed in the back of the mouth. Many sounds are next to impossible to decipher no matter where they originate. For example, 'b', 'p', and 'm' look virtually identical from a lip-reading standpoint. If Ben is one of the men who got a new pen, it's going to take me a while to figure it out. If Mark went to the park, or if mom is the bomb, I'm scratching my head. Is that Matt at bat, or is it Pat? Pass the aspirin, please.

Imagine trying to answer all of your kid's "why" questions in such a manner that he or she can only understand thirty-five percent of what you're saying. Many parents try their best, only to give up in frustration. I've seen it happen many times and it's painful to watch. Instead of genuinely conversing with their deaf children, many parents wave off questions with a *never mind* that makes deaf kids feel they are not important. Some hearing parents respond to their deaf children with terse answers, or just say, "No, don't do that," without explaining why it's not a good idea to shave the cat. No bona fide communication, nothing learned.

Considering most deaf children come from hearing families that do not sign, they probably start their school years having to play catch-up. Their vocabulary base is severely limited as compared to hearing children who can understand and interact with their hearing parents.

My father explained that when he moved to Philadelphia as a teenager, he attended two deaf schools, PSD and the Martin School. Not only did he have to pass the time in classes where he was way ahead of everyone linguistically and academically, but he also had to put up with the then-enforced oral philosophy of both schools. Sign language was forbidden for the same reason the doctors had told my grandparents not to let me use it. It was believed that in order to be successful, all deaf people must speak. This philosophy has thrown a monkey wrench into the academic careers of countless deaf students. Many deaf children have gone through school and learned nothing because they were being trained to be something they simply weren't.

If you had your choice, would you rather that your kid spent six years learning how to successfully pronounce the word "ball", or would you rather that those six years were invested in signing clearly to him the concepts of modern science, literature, and mathematics? This is a no-brainer, right? Guess again. Believe it or not, this argument is still hotly debated. Oralism has worked for some deaf children, and it has ruined the lives of others. It's a very controversial topic.

At PSD, however, the administration and the Deaf community eventually realized that the oral approach resulted in more frustration than success. It was clearly not working with this particular population of deaf students. It was a horror story. My father pointed out how one of his teachers used to hit him on the hands with a ruler whenever he signed—and one day, in total frustration, she actually began smacking him on the ears, hollering, "You can hear! You can hear!"

My dad also told me about his friend Ted who could never learn how to speak no matter how hard he tried. He would put in a good effort but always to no avail. And my father thought it was absolutely disgusting how the teachers would gush, "Oh, that's *wonnndderrrfulll*," whenever Ted managed to emit a guttural sound that bore no resemblance to any spoken word whatsoever.

At times like these, my dad confessed that he often wondered why teachers and administrators couldn't see the obvious. If they would have simply allowed sign language in the classroom, they would have easily covered more material at a much faster rate. Instead,

49

they wasted valuable time trying to pronounce "George Washington" without getting to whatever it was this Mr. Washington had done that was so important.

Regardless, speech was the number one priority throughout my dad's school years. Often, he watched in bemusement as teachers picked on poor Ted. Finally, one of them pushed Ted way beyond the limit of his tolerance. Completely exasperated, Ted cut loose with the one word he could pronounce correctly:

"Fuck!"

My dad did his best to restrain his laughter, lest he wind up on the receiving end of another hard slap. Nonetheless, he was very amused. The teacher didn't know how to react; should she congratulate the boy, or send him to the principal's office? Ted had finally, after all these years, pronounced a word correctly. And it was a word that would have made George Carlin proud. *Wonnndddderrrfulll!*

Neither Ted nor my father would ever forget this special breakthrough. Years later, my dad visited Ted and found that he had an adorable new dog. Ted explained that yes, it was a cute dog and all, but he was irked because his wife had given the dog a name he couldn't pronounce. Ted, going against his wife's wishes, went ahead and named the dog the only thing he could call it.

"Watch this," signed Ted, and with a mischievous smile on his face he took a deep breath.

"Fuck!"

Sure enough, the pooch came bouncing in, his tail wagging affectionately. Never mind that the dog already knew how to respond to several commands *in sign language*. It was only one word, but it was Ted's biggest triumph from the good old oral school days.

Several years after these oral school antics, PSD had a change of philosophy. Sometime in the early '70s they had switched to the use of Total Communication in the classroom, using whichever communication method best met the needs of the students. Most teachers, in my opinion, appeared to use Sim-Com. This involved utilizing spoken words that were supported by their corresponding signs. It was not fluent ASL, but it was a step in the right direction. Students finally had access to a lot more information than they'd ever had before. (Note: later on, a teacher who had been at PSD during both the oral and the TC days confided to me that the students did indeed absorb educational content much faster when sign language was implemented.)

Further on down the road, PSD would eventually adopt a strong philosophy supporting the use of ASL in the classroom. They would take many other steps to close the communication gap, such as implementing a successful Early Intervention Program.

At the point in time when I wanted to transfer, however, the gap was still huge. For even if PSD had improved its communication philosophy in school, there was nothing much it could do to improve things for the students at home and in the outside world. It's been said that ninety-two percent of all learning happens at home, so what can a school do to make up the difference? It's always been a difficult game of catch-up, and probably always will be.

Once my father was done explaining the pitfalls of deaf education, he pointed out that I was lucky to get such a wonderful opportunity at GFS. I was lucky to have had enough residual hearing which allowed me to get by in the hearing world before I went deaf, and I was lucky to have supportive deaf parents after I did. I was lucky to have the cognitive skills to be able to survive at GFS. If he had been given such a choice, my father would have gone with GFS hands down (no pun intended). The education of deaf children still had a long way to go, he explained, so I might as well take advantage of my ability to succeed at GFS. If I had what it took to just barely make it, and it looked like I did, why not just hang in there? Maybe someday, I would

51

learn enough to help turn things around in the deaf world. For now though, the deaf world would have to wait. I wasn't joining it just yet.

After the unsuccessful attempt at convincing my parents to let me transfer, I grudgingly returned to GFS. I cursed my luck. Why couldn't I have been prelingually deaf? Had I been born completely deaf, people would have left me alone. I wouldn't have been in this situation, trying to be the pseudo-hearing person that I was. I didn't fit into the hearing world, and I wasn't allowed to be part of the deaf world; I was too different.

So as my year in the eighth grade drew to a close, I had done it again: By using mirrors, smokescreens and the deadly martial art of Bluff Yu, I had successfully given the impression that I knew and understood most of what was going on. It had grown tiresome. I had especially dreaded Wednesday assemblies where I would sit there bored out of my mind while someone gave a speech, presentation, or a musical performance. Why didn't I just speak up and tell everyone that it was a waste of time? Of course, I never complained. (*Good boy, be hearing.*)

Even if my smile-when-everyone-smiles, laugh-when-everyone-laughs routine gave enough people the impression that I was hearing (or reasonably close), it didn't fool everyone. My teachers were no idiots. They'd been keeping an eye on me all along. They knew I was getting by in my own way, but they also knew it wasn't going to last much longer. While the seventh and eighth grades consisted of mostly hands-on work and following textbook assignments, the ninth through twelfth grades were a whole new ballgame. In those upper grades there would be an emphasis on classroom discussion. Instead of the teacher lecturing and leading us through textbook questions that were easier for me to follow, the whole class would be discussing various topics in depth. We would all be learning from each other. Everyone, that is, except for the deaf guy.

The teachers, however, knew that I was really going to be in a fog if I had to follow an entire classroom discussion on my own. They realized that if I were to remain at GFS, I would need some kind of extra support. Some consultation was done and my mother gave me the news over the summer: I was going to get a sign-language interpreter. My reaction left no doubt about how I felt: *"Noooooooooooooooooo!!!!"*

I went into a big funk over this. It was bad enough that on many occasions, I'd made a fool out of myself trying to act like I knew what was going on. I was a world-champion nodder, saying yes to a lot of things people said in casual conversation. My personal rule was to always say "I don't know" to the teachers and "Yeah" to the students whenever I couldn't understand anything. I thought this was a very efficient way of camouflaging my deafness. Of course, it didn't always work:

"Hey, Mark, how'd you do on the biology test?"

(Smiling) "Yeah!"

"Hey Mark, what time do we have gym today?"

(Smiling) "Yeah!"

"Hey Mark, wanna lick an ashtray?"

(Smiling) "Yeah!"

Despite such incidents, I still believed that most of the time I managed to blend in. With an interpreter though, I was screwed. Everyone would see, every minute of every day, that I was deaf. There was no hiding from this. Everyone would look at me like I was the class freak. I was incredibly self-conscious about this and my self-esteem was beyond shot. It was at an all-time low.

Shortly before the end of the eighth grade, I was informed that I'd been referred to a psychologist. My grade advisor had noted my behavior and my obviously low self-esteem; he'd seen enough to know that such a referral was necessary. Of course, I protested. My mother got the brunt of this. She had to put up with my ranting and raving:

"What am I, nuts? I'm not going to any psychologist. They're for people who are sick in the head. Do I look sick

to you? Psychologists are headshrinkers. What's next, a witch doctor? Booga booga booga. Hey, while you're at it, why not call an exorcist? Aw, man, I wish everyone would just leave me alone. This stinks. They're just sending me there because I'm deaf. They think I'm deaf and dumb. I don't need any help..."

On and on I went, but to no avail. My mother had to drag me there, but off to the psychologist I went.

My first session with the psychologist did not turn out to be the headshrinking, brainpicking session I had feared it would be. Being as self-conscious as I was, I just couldn't stand the thought of sitting with a person whose sole purpose was to analyze me. But my fear immediately turned into a sense of comfort and relief when I found that my psychologist was a caring woman who signed. Seeing that she could sign fluently and that she understood deafness meant a lot to me. I relaxed, and my initial streak of rebelliousness evaporated.

After some small talk and getting to know each other, I was asked to go through some psychological evaluation tests. I went through the usual battery of tests that measured my academic levels as well as my psychological wellbeing. At first I was apprehensive about this, but the psychologist made me feel better by explaining in detail why she had to run me through the whole thing. It meant a lot to me to be able to know exactly what was going on.

"You mean I have to do this to rule out the fact that I might be nuts?" I asked. She grinned, reassured me that I wasn't nuts, and we went on with the testing. As we went through it, I actually began to have fun. I knew I was doing pretty good and just enjoyed it as an opportunity to show off what I could do.

The following week, I beamed with pride as the psychologist told me that my test results were way above average. In fact, she also said that she didn't think I needed to see her much longer. She remarked that she could see how I had accomplished so much against incredible odds, and she respected that. All I really needed, in her opinion, was a pat on the back. Then we moved on to talking about what was going on in school and with my family. I got a lot off my chest: The pressure of trying to be like a hearing person... the embarrassment when I couldn't... being made fun of... and wishing I could be around other deaf who were just like me.

The psychologist acknowledged all of my concerns. For good measure, she told me that she would go over a few things with my family. She'd already noticed that what my grandfather told her about me was completely different from what she saw with her own eyes. My grandfather had painted a bleak picture of how I was not good enough at several things, particularly speech. The psychologist informed me that my speech was far better than what she'd been led to expect, but that was irrelevant. The important thing was that my grandparents needed to acknowledge that I was deaf, and that I was doing incredibly well considering the circumstances. My grades were better than a lot of hearing students, but to my grandfather it wasn't enough. During report card time, he would grill me on every teacher's written comments about how I needed to sit up closer, wear my hearing aid more, and be more involved in class discussion. Never mind how good my grades were; I needed to be more hearing.

By no means am I advocating a parenting philosophy of, "Oh, don't be so hard on him, he's deaf." Anything but. In situations where a teacher reported that I didn't give enough effort on a certain project, or failed to study enough for a final exam, the admonitions I got for it were appropriately called for. But there were some reprimands that I did not deserve, reprimands based on comments such as the following examples (actual quotes from some of my report cards):

"I would have liked seeing Mark make greater contribution to class discussion."

"He does not keep track of where we are in discussion."

55

"I urge Mark to sit up front, focus his attention . . ."

Although there were many positive comments in my report cards where the teachers acknowledged I had overcome a lot of adversity, my grandfather always gave me a hard time about my lack of involvement in class discussion. Sure, I'm grateful he pushed me hard academically, for it enabled me to set higher standards for myself; his only mistake was in pushing me to be more hearing. That would accomplish nothing, except for maybe turning me into a neurotic.

And then..., shortly before the ninth grade began, I was at my grandparent's apartment when my grandfather called me into the den for yet another private conversation. We'd had countless meetings like this before, and I grew to detest them. But this time it was different.

"Mark," he began, "this year is going to be a challenge for you. You've got a lot going on, but you've accomplished more than many people thought possible. I just wanted to say that you've proven yourself quite well. I'm not going to bother you anymore about GFS, Mark. You're on your own now."

I was completely surprised. It was a complete turnaround from what I would have expected from him. Although in general he was a fun guy to be with, as far as school was concerned he had always been dead serious. Perhaps he felt that I needed to be ten times better than everyone else in order to compensate for my deafness. Whatever it was, it was a big, unexpected surprise when he told me I was on my own. If I had any problems and needed advice, of course he would be there. If I ever turned in a lousy report card, then it would be up to my deaf parents to say something (as it should be). Now my grandfather could go back to being just that, a grandfather. The same went for my grandmother, who had also shown a considerable amount of worry and concern over my academics. Our relationship greatly improved after this announcement—I could go back to enjoying their company without rolling my eyes whenever a school-related issue came up.

When I rode back home with my mother that afternoon, she explained the reason behind what had just happened. The psychologist had actually called my grandfather for a private discussion of their own. Basically, she told him to wake up and smell the roses. He'd been so worried about my deafness that he had failed to see the big picture: Overall, I was doing pretty well. With all that said and done, I felt vindicated.

"See? I *told* you I wasn't nuts."

7

::

ow that I could move on and face further academic challenges that awaited at GFS, there was one more obstacle that needed to be dealt with. I needed to overcome all fear and self-doubt. Despite reassurances from various adults, I still wasn't comfortable with the idea of a sign language interpreter in class. Luckily for me, I got a brief reprieve. An interpreter was not immediately available when the ninth grade began. A red-tape snafu had bought me some extra time. It gave me time to assess the situation, the people around me, and how we would all respond to this person who would follow me around like a parole officer. It gave me more time to struggle with my deafness in my own little solitary world.

And struggle with my deafness I did, in strange ways indeed. I immediately found out that the required ninth grade music class was not going to be a piece of cake. Previously, from third grade at Plymouth Meeting up to eighth grade at GFS, I could just barely get by in choir. I had enough residual hearing so that with a music sheet I could learn the words to most songs. My sensorineural deafness was such that everyone's voice was garbled to me—but with the lyrics in my hand, I knew in advance what everyone was singing.

Usually, I could follow the music well enough to learn the words. And then I would dazzle all the girls in the audience with my sexy baritone as I belted one tune after the other and—*what are you, nuts? Of course, I lip-synched.* I faked my way through choir for *years*. As crazy as this seems, sometimes it was actually fun. At PMFS I had actually looked forward to the special events where we performed for our parents and friends.

The ninth grade was a different story; this was the big leagues. Instead of one class of fifteen kids singing together, the ninth grade choir was the entire class—all 104 of us. To make matters worse, the teachers split us up into different sections: tenor, bass, soprano, and terrified deaf kid. I was completely lost. There was no way I could keep up with all of this. After attending about three classes, I gave up. From there on, I cut weekly choir class, choosing instead to hide in some remote spot in the library. I would spend that time catching up on my homework, all the while hoping I wouldn't get in trouble for cutting choir. When the ninth grade gave a performance during an assembly, I sheepishly sat with the eighth graders and hoped no one would notice.

Again, we have a similar issue reappearing here: Why didn't I speak up? I could have and should have told them that it was crazy to put a deaf guy in choir class. Who would dispute that? What were they going to do, put me up front and make me do an ear-splitting solo rendition of *Ain't No Mountain High Enough*? Of course not. But I was convinced that because I was isolated in the hearing world, I had to play by the hearing rules. I never complained.

Finally, a couple of months into the ninth grade, the charade would end. I was informed that an interpreter would soon be joining me in class. This was it; all fingers would be pointed in my direction. *See that guy? He's deaf.* They were all going to make fun of me, and I cringed just thinking about it. Remember how I was ashamed of my hearing aid in grade school? At least I could conceal that little contraption behind my ear. Where was I going to stash the interpreter?

The weekend before my interpreter's debut, I decided to do some soul-searching and wound up reading the entire school directory. I sifted through all the names so that I could assess who would be most likely to ridicule me. From there, I would figure out a way to deal with whatever humiliation they would heap on my fragile deaf psyche. I shuffled through the pages with trepidation.

"Allen... nah. Brown... nah." A few minutes later it was, "Zimmerman... nah." Suddenly, it dawned on me. Because of communication barriers I wasn't really close to my classmates—but no one out there was making my life miserable, either. They were pretty much leaving me alone. It was not they, the other students, but I alone who needed to come to terms with my deafness. I realized that I was being way too self-conscious. It was time to give my classmates a chance to see who I really was. Most importantly, it was time to give myself a chance, a chance to be deaf.

The following Monday, I was in my usual fog in history class. A stimulating classroom discussion was underway, but I was sitting in the corner biting my nails and drawing doodles in my notebook. To give the teacher a sense that I was hanging in there as best as I could, I would occasionally look at whoever was talking. It might have looked like I was following the conversation, but in reality I was in my own world. *Two outs, bases loaded... bottom of the ninth... seventh game of the World Series. It doesn't get any better than this! Up to the plate steps Mark Drolsbaugh, the last hope for the Philadelphia Phillies... and here's the pitch. . . .*

My daydream was suddenly interrupted by the class advisor, who entered the classroom with another adult. He discreetly pointed in my direction and all of a sudden, this woman pulls up a chair and sits very close to me. Very close. What the hell was this? She was right in my face, slowly enunciating with her lips every word of the classroom discussion. I was utterly confused. *Where was the sign language?* They hired some idiot who slowly repeated everything with exaggerated lip movements!

To make matters worse, she leaned so close to me that we looked like two lovesick teenagers sharing a sundae in a '50s malt shop. My face reddened with embarrassment as I put up with this cheap imitation

60

of an interpreter for another half-hour. I could feel the rest of the class sneaking glances at us and wondering, *What the hell is that?*

Mercifully, the class finally came to an end and my interpreter was formally able to introduce herself.

"Hi, my name is Emily. Sorry I was late, but I had a meeting with your advisor for a while. I will be working with you from now on." She was really nice, but . . .

"Hi," I said, somewhat hesitantly. Then I began to sign slowly, "Nice to meet you."

Emily's eyes widened in astonishment. Signing fluently, she asked, *"You sign?* Oh my god! No one told me! This is unbelievable!" She dropped her head on the desk and started laughing. Looking up, she explained that she was given the impression that I was a total oralist who did not know any sign language whatsoever. I explained to her that I was never encouraged to sign, but was able to gradually pick up ASL from my parents and my friends at PSD. Emily shook her head, smiling, and we laughed at the whole thing. We continued signing to each other and I realized that for the first time in my career at GFS, I was having a lengthy, meaningful conversation with someone.

At the next class, Emily signed full speed ahead and the entire class was mesmerized. *Teacher? What teacher? Look at those beautiful hands!* The beauty of ASL was there for all to see—graceful, flowing hands relaying tons of information to a totally awed deaf student. There was certainly nothing to be embarrassed about as far as I was concerned. In fact, I was too much in awe of all the information that Emily was able to relay in sign language. Wonder of wonders, I found that my classmates were pretty cool people, after all! I suddenly had access to their classroom discussion as well as their casual conversation and jokes. For the first time, I could understand everything that went on around me and I could appreciate everyone's input. You know how they say two minds are better than one? Suddenly I had access to 104 minds. It was a

61

veritable orgy of information. How could I have gone for so long, while missing out on so much?

My life had changed incredibly for the better after I got the interpreter. The same went for my teachers, who knew they could now treat me as an equal; the old *Duh, I didn't know there was a homework assignment* excuse didn't work anymore. I was in on everything, and I benefited from it immensely. Not only was I expected to improve my work (I did), but I was also expected to be involved in classroom discussion (I was).

Other students were able to develop a better understanding of who I was. Now they realized why I had appeared so lost (not to mention weird) in earlier times. Some of them were so impressed with sign language that they were inspired to learn some themselves. There were actually students who learned enough so that they could hold a very basic conversation in ASL, although most just learned how to fingerspell the alphabet. But whether it was signing words or fingerspelling them, it meant a lot to me. It was great to see how other students were eager to understand my world.

One such student, Erik, helped other students become more sensitive to my needs. One day I was sitting with a small group of classmates in the cafeteria, and I was completely out of it. There was just no way I could keep up with the conversation. Erik eventually joined us at our table and he noticed right away that I was not able to hold my own in a group discussion. At first he briefly took on the role of interpreter, summarizing the content of the other students' dialogue. It didn't appeal to either of us, so we started having our own conversation in ASL as the others continued speaking amongst themselves. At that moment one of the students sitting next to Erik began to protest.

"Hey," he interrupted. "It's not fair when you two sign like that. I can't understand what you're saying."

Erik couldn't believe this. He shot back with an incredulous look.

"How do you think *Mark* feels, twenty-four hours a day, when he can't understand anything you and everyone else are saying?"

The object of Erik's wrath suddenly had a blank look on his face. The reality of the situation hit him. Boom! Massive insight in progress.

"Holy crap..., you're right."

Soon afterward, this student went out and learned sign language himself. So did a number of others at the table that day. It was a tremendous reality check for them. When my interpreter heard about what had happened, she broke into a big grin. She knew we were all learning something new. Before long, a number of students would be asking her for feedback on their signing skills. This whole thing was a blessing for me, indeed.

Although Emily did a fantastic job, this was not a long-term gig for her and soon she moved out of town to pursue other opportunities. Another interpreter, Deborah, was hired in her place. Not only was Deb as fluent in ASL, but she was also like a walking encyclopedia; anything there was to know about the culturally Deaf world, you name it, she knew it. It was strange, but here was this hearing person teaching me, a deaf guy, everything I had ever wanted to know about ASL and Deaf culture. We would talk about various deaf topics, and she would point out things I'd never had the time or the maturity to realize on my own. In addition, I noticed that having an interpreter around actually improved my own signing skills. I was consistently exposed to ASL every day and I absorbed it like a sponge. I was learning more about myself and enjoying my education as well.

Finally, after stumbling around for the first couple of years, I was genuinely enjoying myself at GFS. Perhaps one of the funniest stories was the time Mr. Gratwick, my eleventh grade history teacher, kept me after class. History was my worst subject and it was kind of awkward because Mr. Gratwick was also the varsity baseball coach. I dreaded him during the morning, and loved him in the afternoon. One day, history class had just ended and I made a beeline for the door. At the last second Mr. Gratwick stepped up and asked if I could stay for a few minutes. Uh-oh. I knew I'd bombed on a recent assignment, and apparently it was time to face the music. I braced myself for an impromptu history lecture. Instead, to my surprise, this after class meeting was about baseball.

"Mark," Mr. Gratwick began, "I need to go over something that happened in yesterday's game." My eyes lit up. For baseball, I had all the time in the world.

"When you were at bat with Tommy on third, I gave you the signal for a squeeze bunt. You missed it and Tommy nearly got picked off. Are you sure you know the bunt sign?" I acknowledged that I did, but in that particular situation I must have been distracted or something. It was just a mental error on my part. Mr. Gratwick said it was all right; he just wanted to be sure I knew all of the signals. Then he broke into a big grin.

"You, of all people, missing a sign!"

Now that I was settled down at GFS and enjoying school for a change, it was time to move on to other things that appeal to teenagers. I was ready to grow up, meet some girls, and get a life. Thanks to my interpreter at school and baseball at home, getting a life was the easy part. I had a number of new friends at school who accepted me for who I was, and at home I grew closer to friends with whom I'd spent entire summers playing baseball.

As for meeting girls—that was a total bust. Yes, there were a number of girls who would say hello or even be platonic friends, but none of them wanted anything beyond that. I was the deaf nice guy. Nice but, well, *deaf*. Reasonably fun to talk to, nice to get to know a bit better, but not someone you would want to bring home with you. I'm not exactly sure what it was. Maybe none of the girls wanted to date a deaf guy because they preferred the popular jocks. Maybe some girls were actually interested, but uncertain about how to connect with someone who was so different. Maybe I was just a nerd in general, regardless of whether or not I was deaf.

Whatever it was, it got frustrating at times. I saw plenty of guys getting all the girls they wanted. Some of them seemed to have girls coming and going through a revolving door. But not me. I scratched my head in bewilderment as everyone else got all the action. What was wrong with me?

In some ways this was a blessing. Someday, when pigs flew and hell froze over, I would have a girlfriend. And when I did, I would appreciate it more. I knew I wouldn't date and throw girls away like they were the latest flavor of the month. I'd never take any woman for granted, that was for sure.

Finally, one day a pig flew by my window and a girl named Karen asked me if I would accompany her to her junior prom. It caught me completely off guard and I had to ask her to repeat the question for something like nine times to make sure this wasn't a cruel joke.

Karen was not from GFS, I didn't really know her, and she asked me totally out of the blue. She was the friend of the girlfriend of a good friend of mine, and she'd heard I was wallowing in miser..., uh, she'd heard I was one of the most eligible bachelors in town. Further throwing me for a loop was the fact that prior to asking me to do this, she had practiced repeatedly until she could ask in sign language. Who was this girl? Why me? Why now? *Why not?* I said yes. It'd been far too long since I'd had an opportunity like this.

It was definitely worth the wait. We had a great time at the prom and kept seeing each other for a long time afterward. It turned out to be one hell of a learning experience, in more ways than one.

Of course, my parents were elated that I finally had a girlfriend; my dad was glad to know that I wasn't the eunuch he thought I was, and my mom was absolutely

65

thrilled that there was someone for me who knew sign language. As long as Karen could sign, that was all that mattered.

Unfortunately, the rest of my family was not as receptive. Karen was a fluent signer, yes, but she was also Catholic. Needless to say, they were not too thrilled about it and they let me know.

All of this had me terribly confused. After years of being a total zero on the dating scene, I'd finally found someone who not only wanted to know me on an intimate level, but also knew sign language to boot. Was I supposed to throw it all away just because she was Catholic? I didn't understand the big deal. This was going to be a lesson for me, similar to the one I'd learned while growing up with Sekou: Why should anyone's religion or race make a difference in how we get along?

Neither religion nor race mattered to me, but communication did. If you were willing to be my friend and accept my deafness, I didn't care if you were white, black, Catholic, Jewish, Swahili, or whatever. I didn't care if you worked as a CEO or passed your time handing out flowers at the airport. If you can *communicate*, you're my friend. This is a great example of how I feel that my deafness has helped me grow spiritually—I could appreciate my interaction with anyone, and just be happy we could get along rather than get bogged down on whatever groups or religions they belonged to. Really, human interaction is a blessing; it is such a waste to discriminate.

As I came to terms with my hearing family's initial reaction to Karen's background (they eventually warmed up to her), I took advantage of the opportunity to find out just what the big deal was supposed to be. Out of curiosity, I began attending church with Karen. It was a brand new experience and it was awesome. My parents didn't really object, but they were concerned that it would greatly upset my mother's family. I agreed with them on this so I never mentioned it to anyone other than my parents.

Hey, it was my business. And I looked at it this way: If Karen could jump so deeply into my world of sign language, I could likewise jump into her world of Catholicism. Why not? We should all learn from one another. I really believe I had a good thing going. Both Judaism and Catholicism are beautiful religions, and I was in this unique situation where I could experience both. Hanukkah, Christmas, the whole shebang, it was all good. No big deal. After all, I had already celebrated Christmas on many occasions with my father's family. How could it hurt if I was involved with one more? I had the best of both worlds.

As it turned out, I enjoyed going to church and learned a lot from it. What really helped was the fact that Karen would discreetly interpret everything into sign language. I had access and I was fascinated. I was not only struck by the differences between Catholicism and Judaism, but even more so by their similarities. There were common threads everywhere and I noticed this every week. It reinforced a sense that somehow, we're all in this together.

My only problem with religion, then, was the confusion I felt after seeing so many people making a fuss over their religious differences. I never mentioned my church experiences to my Jewish family, for I had seen their reservations about my dating a Catholic girl. Likewise, I rarely talked about Jewish culture in the presence of Catholics, for I had noticed a sense of anti-Semitism in certain individuals. Maybe it was just me, but I felt a distinctive sense of us versus them. Although most of the people and most of the experiences were overwhelmingly positive, there were always people on each side making derogatory comments about other faiths. Whenever this happened I instinctively knew it was wrong. Both religions, in my opinion, are beautiful in their own right. I guess we all have an individual responsibility to learn tolerance and respect for each other. Until that happens, we all have a long way to go.

In a strange way, I'm actually glad I'm deaf. Perhaps if I weren't deaf, I might have developed a true bias favoring the first religion I was exposed to. Perhaps if I were hearing, the first morsel of religious dogma thrown my way might have been unconditionally accepted as Absolute Truth.

But no, I was deaf. I grew up with a blank slate that allowed me to see things from a more neutral perspective. In other words, deafness emptied my cup. Thanks to deafness I can see the different religions simply as they are, without any bias. It has helped me learn so much about people—both the good and the bad— and I literally thank God for deafness.

Karen and I had a long relationship, dating each other exclusively for about three years. *Three years!* Normally, three years are not much. But when those years are ages sixteen, seventeen, and eighteen, it's an eternity. In all honesty, one year probably would have been enough. The years sixteen, seventeen, and eighteen are best suited for dating different people, socializing, and learning the responsibilities that come with an approaching adulthood.

For Karen and me it was a different story. Whereas other teenage couples routinely broke up and found new people to go out with, I held on to Karen with a viselike grip. After all, she was the only girl in the whole neighborhood who signed. If we broke up, I knew it would take me *years* to find another language-accessible girlfriend. So I held on to her, through good times and bad. Sometimes *really* bad. We could barely tolerate each other near the end of our relationship yet at the same time it was hard to let go. On top of that, I had a ridiculous level of insecurity that was not conducive to a healthy relationship. I always felt that hearing guys had much more to offer than I did, and I was afraid that sooner or later Karen would find out. Sure enough, Karen would inevitably be ready to go her own way. But she also felt bad for me and I could understand her mixed emotions.

The end came after Karen enrolled in a local college. After years of being in an all-girls' high school, she was surrounded by other men for the first time in her life. They were hearing, like her, and shared similar interests in music and entertainment that I could not. In fact, Karen remarked frequently that she felt guilty whenever we went to the movies because she knew she could never fully interpret the mood and context that was taking place on the screen. Likewise, I would spend hours in movie theaters pretending I was enjoying every moment because I wanted her to be happy. It was not fair to either of us. We knew it had to end, and we appropriately broke up. For Karen, it meant she was free at last. For me, it meant the same thing, although I was too heartbroken at the time to realize it.

Breaking up with Karen was just the tip of the iceberg. An awful lot of transitions were in store. In the spring of 1984, I was a senior at GFS and graduation was right around the corner. The first deaf student ever to graduate from GFS! Sadly though, it was around this time when Grandpop was losing a tough battle against cancer. He was hospitalized in such bad shape that we weren't sure he would last long enough to see me graduate. It had been his big dream that I would succeed at GFS, a dream that would soon become reality.

By late April, Grandpop was quickly running out of precious time. More than anything, I wanted him to know that a GFS diploma was in the bag. I approached him in his hospital room and informed him that not only was I going to graduate in June, but I had also been accepted into Temple University. For whatever reason, I also told him I was going to be an accountant. I have no idea why I said that. I guess it seemed to be the right thing to do. Everyone else in my hearing family was a successful doctor, lawyer, accountant, or teacher, so I didn't want Grandpop to get

69

the impression that I had no direction in life. I thought it would be best to let him die happy knowing that not only was I on track to be the first deaf graduate of GFS, but that I also had a prospective career in business.

Finally, on May 4, 1984, my dad woke me up at six a.m. with the devastating news that Grandpop had passed on. The most spiritual person I had ever known was gone. After a brief trip to the hospital with the family, I returned to GFS around noon, totally numb from the immeasurable loss. It was just too surreal. I couldn't believe Grandpop had actually died.

As shell-shocked as I was, there was still a baseball game to be played later on that day against Archbishop Ryan, one of the toughest teams on our schedule. I wasn't sure if I should play or not. But then again, I recalled how Grandpop had always been a familiar face at many of my games. He was my biggest fan, always cheering me on. So that was settled; I was going to play this one for Grandpop.

When the game rolled around, Archbishop Ryan jumped to a big lead in the first two innings. They were up 5-0 when Mr. Gratwick decided to pull our starting pitcher and put me on the mound. This was clearly the strongest team we had to play all year and we were simply outmatched that day. Nonetheless, I pitched five innings, getting seven strikeouts while giving up only two earned runs. While I may have had better statistics in other games, I would say this was the best I had ever pitched in my life, considering the circumstances and the talent level of the other team. We may have lost the game but the experience toughened us up for the stretch run. We steamrolled to an overall 19-4 record and won the Friends' League Championship a few weeks later. And shortly afterwards, I had a diploma in my hand. This one's for you, Grandpop.

It was hard getting used to life without Grandpop. He'd been my biggest role model, one of the few people I could really look up to. Granted, there was much he did not understand about deafness but he made up for it in so many other ways. I considered myself blessed to have had such a wonderful grandfather and I realized there was much I had taken for granted. With that in mind, I decided I would make the most of the time I had left to spend with my surviving grandparents.

Considering that my dad's mother, Nana, had moved from Scranton to an apartment in nearby Hatboro (with her second husband Mike Novak), I took advantage of the opportunity to visit them often. Most of the time, I would accompany my parents to visit Nana and Mike on some weekends and during holidays such as Christmas and Easter. After Grandpop died, however, I got into the habit of driving over myself, just to say hello and shoot the breeze.

I might have been a young adolescent and barely old enough to have a driver's license, but I still noticed that there were certain differences in family dynamics that stood out when I interacted with my deaf grandparents. For instance, I was incredibly relaxed with them. It was just kicking back, no pressure; no struggling to read lips; no need to act like a hearing person. There were no reminders that I needed to speak more clearly or wear a hearing aid. With Nana and Mike, this was not necessary. They were deaf themselves... *and they understood.*

If I told them about a time I completely screwed up in class, they would acknowledge that it must have been hard for me. (My hearing relatives usually told me it was my responsibility to sit up front.) If it was something amusing, such as the time I said "I don't know" to the substitute teacher who asked me what my name was, Nana and Mike laughed along with me. I appreciated this, because although there are many situations where there's nothing more we can do but laugh at ourselves, deafness was no laughing matter for my hearing family. Worrying about me to a fault, they would react with grave concern, and repeatedly pointed out that I would have to make certain adjustments to survive in the hearing world.

71

To Nana and Mike, however, deafness was something we were, not something that needed to be fixed. Consequently, I never felt like I needed to win their approval. Nana and Mike didn't care if I wore a hearing aid; they didn't care if I could speak clearly or not. They didn't worry incessantly about things that were out of our control. There was no "You should know this" or "You should do that." Whoever I was at that particular moment in time was just fine with them. The important thing was that I was doing okay in whatever way I could.

Another benefit of having deaf family members was that with them, there was no Dinner Table Syndrome where the deaf person sits completely lost amongst the hearing family members that are having a table conversation. So it was not uncommon for my parents and I to stay for a duration of time which would have been unbearable with hearing people. Time flew quickly because everyone was fully involved in whatever was going on.

One evening in 1985, I paid a visit to my deaf grandparents and enjoyed a lengthy stay. Around ten p.m. it was time to go, so I said goodbye and headed out to the parking lot. As I pulled out of my parking space, I looked up and could see Nana standing by the window of the eighth floor lobby. There was something surreal about it that froze me in my tracks. I could only see her silhouette eight stories up, and it seemed like time slowed down as her hand gently waved goodbye. I waved back and found myself overcome with emotion. For whatever reason, I was all choked up. Tears actually streamed down my face.

I really believe that somehow, Nana and I both knew that this was the last time things would be the way they were. I couldn't understand for the life of me why I started sniffling as she waved goodbye. But somehow, deep down I knew. So did Nana. Call me weird, but sometimes it seems like life is one big stage and we're all actors following a script. It was like subconsciously, Nana and I knew what was next in our life drama. Whatever it was, something was definitely up. Nana had never walked to the lobby and waved from the window before. The hair on the back of my neck stood up and I was overwhelmed by a sense of imminent change.

The following day I had my answer. The phone rang, and it was a relative calling to inform us that Nana had suffered a nasty stroke. She would never be the same again. Visiting her in the hospital, my family and I discovered that she was unable to walk, unable to use her right hand, had lost her ability to read, and was confusing various relatives' names. She referred to my dad as "Robert", and Uncle Bob as "Charlie". She was in for a long period of rehabilitation.

As often as I could, I visited Nana in the hospital. Perhaps I felt guilty because when Grandpop had been terminally ill, I was not always there for him. It was impossible for me to be involved as much as I would have liked. Family members shielded me from the grim nature of his terminal illness for as long as possible, and even after it became obvious, there were people telling me what to say or do.

Now that it was Nana who was sick, I was saying the things that came from my heart. Perhaps I was more mature this time around, or perhaps I was more comfortable in the presence deaf relatives. We openly shared stories with Nana, and we discussed her progress with the doctors. With Grandpop, I was often in the dark as far as what the doctors and relatives said. Sometimes I felt like a burden, for it was hard enough for the hearing family to deal with Grandpop's illness without having to slowly repeat the dismal news to me. With Nana, however, most of us were deaf, so we were all on the same page and shared the medical prognosis together. We had the whole story, which was the fact that she had quite an uphill battle to fight.

Slowly, Nana began to make enough progress so that she could be discharged from the hospital. But before returning home, she would have to spend some time in

73

a rehabilitation center. This turned out to be Hopkins House in Jenkintown. It was a fine facility and Nana did indeed make some progress. She slowly regained her ability to walk, although she would still need to spend much time in a wheelchair.

Everything else, however, came along slowly. Her right hand was still curled up, unable to function normally. She complained that she could no longer read books or follow the captions on TV. Interestingly, her signing skills remained intact, although she was limited to signing with one hand. (A report in *Time* magazine several years later would confirm that sign language stimulates different areas of the brain than the ones activated by spoken and written language.)

Shortly after returning home, Nana had yet another setback. She collapsed from a second stroke, and Mike was barely able to assist her in time to save her life. After another hospital stay, it was determined that Nana would need to live in a place where she could have round-the-clock medical supervision. Grudgingly, she and Mike accepted the family's strong recommendation that they move to the Nevil Home, a nursing home for the deaf in Media, Pennsylvania.

Of course, no couple likes to leave the freedom of their own place to live in, of all places, a nursing home. Nana might have lost some function, but her wits were still intact:

"Put me out to pasture, eh? Why not take me behind the barn and shoot me?"

Soon, however, Nana and Mike were settled down and having a great time. There were nightly events featuring movies, games, and occasional trips such as an excursion to Atlantic City. The other residents were deaf and most of the staff signed, so Nana and Mike were actually socializing a whole lot more than they ever had at their old apartment complex.

Gradually, Nana regained that old spark we hadn't seen in her for a long time. She started hurling friendly

74

insults at Mike, and even threw the Kleenex box at him whenever he dozed off in front of the TV. When she started making fun of other people and cracking one-liners, a la the Sophia character on *The Golden Girls*, that's when I knew she was on her way back. She would jokingly complain that Mike had a roving eye for the other ladies. ("Eighty years old and he wants to be a swinger!") Mike would play along mischievously, making catcalls whenever a female resident walked by their room.

It turned into one big party. It even reached the point where our family smuggled in beer and whiskey for Mike. It wasn't permitted, but so what. If these were the twilight years, why shouldn't they enjoy every minute of it?

Although Nana would never be exactly the same as she was before the strokes, the progress she made at the Nevil Home was amazing. I couldn't help but notice. At the Hopkins House, she was surrounded by the most professional, competent staff of physical therapists you could ever ask for, yet her heart wasn't really in it. She made enough progress to go home, but just barely. At the Nevil Home, Nana clearly enjoyed life again and practically turned into a party animal. Her spirits, remarkably, rose high enough that she was able to bounce back considerably from her stroke. I really believe that having deaf friends, family, and ASL-competent staff around her gave Nana the emotional boost that enabled her to regain much of what she had lost.

It wasn't long before she was once again able to read and do her favorite crossword puzzles. Yes, she still had to spend much time in a wheelchair and she also struggled with her short-term memory. But nonetheless, she had still come a long way. It was a remarkable comeback. The bottom line was, once again she was enjoying a quality of life she hadn't experienced since her days as the cook at a local deaf club.

If you stop to think about it, you'll notice a parallel here: Often, deaf advocates have argued that deaf children deserve the quality of life that is available to them when you allow them interact with their deaf peers. In this case, with Nana and Mike, I had discovered that it was a universal truth that applied to all ages. (Ironically, I had yet to realize that this truth applied to me as well.) The Nevil Home allowed them to rediscover that missing spark, a spark that gave them strength to recover physically, emotionally, and spiritually.

Nana and Mike would spend the next seven years in the Nevil Home, where the family would get together to celebrate Christmas and other joyous occasions on a regular basis. When they both eventually passed away within months of each other (Nana in the fall of 1991, and Mike in the spring of 1992), we had accumulated many wonderful memories. Interestingly, when they passed away, I did not grieve as hard as I had when Grandpop died in 1984. Maybe it was because Grandpop had such a powerful influence on me that it was like losing a part of myself. Maybe it was because Nana and Mike had often frankly discussed with the family how they were ready to die—it gave us all an opportunity to make the most of the final years and to have closure. Nana and Mike gave us all plenty of time to say what needed to be said and to do what needed to be done. It was like a peaceful send-off to the next world for them. So perhaps we were more prepared to deal with their departure. Either way, I do miss them very much and consider myself blessed to have had such wonderful grandparents on both sides of the family.

8

∶ ∶

Despite graduating from what was one of the best schools in Philadelphia, somewhere down the line I forgot to pat myself on the back. My self-esteem, somehow, gradually slipped back down to rock bottom. I may have graduated from a school where many graduates went on to success in Ivy League colleges, but I didn't dare dream of such lofty ideals. Rather than Doogie Howser, M.D., I was going to be Homer Simpson. For as much as I knew that I had made it through one of the toughest academic environments in town, I hadn't seen any other deaf role models around.

Apparently, being the first deaf guy to graduate from GFS had both positive and negative implications. On the one hand, I had accomplished something that was once considered impossible, and that certainly was commendable. On the other hand, I was in uncharted territory. I had no deaf role models to follow. Where was I supposed to go from here? I had no idea. My hearing classmates may have gone on to medical school or various prestigious positions in science, business, and entertainment, but they were *hearing*. What was a deaf guy to do?

In a way, I was the victim of a self-imposed glass ceiling. I surmised that my hearing classmates were of course going to be successful, because they were hearing. They had the leadership qualities; I didn't. I may have improved after getting an interpreter, but I was still a few steps behind; being a leader was out of the question. If there were situations where a good idea was needed, someone else had already come up with the solution by the time the problem was effectively communicated to me through the interpreter. Lots of times, I would raise my hand two or three seconds after everyone else due to this small delay, and then curse under my breath as the teacher called on some other student who gave precisely the same answer that I'd planned to share. Train gone, sorry. I was close, but never equal.

Not being equal to anyone gave me an excuse to sell myself short. My breakup with Karen further reinforced my belief that a deaf guy just didn't have much of a fair shot at succeeding in the hearing world. Although we managed to remain friends, it was painful at first to see how easily Karen met and dated other men. She was having the time of her life with hearing guys who had much more to offer than I ever could, and I was back to striking out with the ladies. I was going nowhere fast. I had no dreams or aspirations. If I landed any job at all, be it flipping burgers at McDonald's or washing windshields with a squeegee at street intersections, it would be *not bad for a deaf guy*.

Eventually I got a part-time job as a supermarket clerk. It was okay, nothing fancy. To me, it was the end of the road. Since this job was *not bad for a deaf guy*, I made it my career goal. Maybe someday I could manage the general merchandise department, who knows. Even if that never happened, I was still doing pretty good— because, everybody, sing along with me: *Not bad for a deaf guy*.

Needless to say, this was probably the lowest point of my life. Grandpop was gone, my love life was non-existent, and I was in a rut while stocking the same shelves every day at work. There had to be more to life than this. Something was missing, and I grew tired of this horribly empty feeling. If I'd had any guts I would have uprooted and started all over someplace else. In fact, I mentioned this to some of my hearing friends at a party one evening. I told them that I'd heard of this place called NTID (National Technical Institute for the Deaf) in Rochester, and was thinking of going there. Perhaps it was time to move on and hang out with people like myself for a change. But it never happened. Not only were my friends able to talk me out of it, I didn't think I was ready for such a move yet anyway. I was in a rut, but it was a *comfortable* rut in the hometown I had lived in all my life.

One of my friends told me that I didn't need to look elsewhere for happiness; I simply needed to look inward and find more confidence. I needed to be more assertive, needed to believe in myself. Only then would things start looking up. He definitely had a good point there; I was in dire need of an attitude overhaul.

After some soul-searching, I found an intriguing answer: The martial arts. This was not entirely out of the blue; I had taken Shotokan a few years earlier, and it had left an indelible impression. I remembered how I'd always looked forward to class, and I realized that the martial arts had this knack for filling a gap in my life. What did I have to lose? Perhaps it was time to start up again. After checking out some of the schools in my neighborhood, I decided to enroll at a Tae Kwon Do school in nearby Willow Grove. Not surprisingly, it turned out to be a valuable experience.

First and foremost, Tae Kwon Do (as well as any other martial art) is physically relaxing and cathartic. If you have any pent-up stress or frustration, this is the perfect outlet. Not only do you release negative tension but you also pick up positive vibes from your teachers and students when you work out in harmony. You develop an ability to focus and stay tuned to the present moment, which is the key to inner peace. It does wonders for your state of mind.

Not long after taking up Tae Kwon Do, the difference in the way I carried myself was noticeable. In fact, the two times that I had to take an extended leave of absence from my training (once for a hernia operation, and again after a freak surfing accident), my boss at work observed a big difference in my usually calm demeanor; my tolerance level in difficult situations had waned somewhat, compared to when I regularly participated in Tae Kwon Do.

On a different level, Tae Kwon Do improved my self-esteem. When I started my training, I noticed that the advanced students looked awesome as they executed difficult techniques with smooth precision. I couldn't believe that someday I, too, would be performing the same complex routines. Sure enough, as time went by I improved, and I realized I could routinely accomplish what I had once thought was impossible. It taught me the value of patience and perseverance.

If at this point it appears that I'm getting too big for my britches regarding martial arts skills, hang on a second. That also is naturally taken care of by the rigors of training. When I was a green belt—about intermediate level—I began thinking that maybe I was the Second Coming of Bruce Lee. This is understandable because it is at this stage when beginners start to become adept at all of the basic techniques. Instead of awkward, off-balance kicks, I began to deliver powerful blows with speed and accuracy. *Whoooooomp!* I could literally feel the energy surging through me. Damn, I was good. Or so I thought.

Eventually, I worked my way up to the more advanced level of red belt. All of the hard work was paying off, as I was able to master the more difficult techniques and soon would be testing for black belt. I was warming up one day, when I noticed one of the green belts going through his repertoire of kicks and punches.

Hmmm, I thought. *He's pretty good, but he's got a long way to go.*

All of a sudden, at that moment, it hit me. I realized that statement not only applied to the green belt, but to me as well. As a green belt I thought I knew everything; as a red belt I knew, in retrospect, that I was wrong. Not only that, I realized that at the present moment, even as a red belt I still knew nothing compared to what was ahead. And of course, as a black belt I would likewise know nothing compared to the path beyond. It was a humbling insight.

Once you get such insights from your training it adds a spiritual dimension to your life. You begin to question the meaning of some things, and you realize that you have a power deep inside you that you were never aware of before. I think we all have this power. It lies dormant within us, patiently waiting until we're ready to wake up and kick some butt. We all have more ability and wisdom than we give ourselves credit for—it just takes a certain amount of self-actualization before one is ready to unleash it.

Once I realized this, I turned into an Eastern Philosophy enthusiast. I read everything I could get my hands on about Zen Buddhism, Taoism, and all sorts of spiritual literature. I became a strong believer in the inner voice, an insight junkie. Anytime there was a moment of inspiration, of wordless understanding where things just somehow made sense, a light bulb clicked on in my head. Mmm, brain candy. I wanted more, more, more. And all it took was a few quiet moments of introspection.

Ironically, during my school years I had been cultivating an awareness of the inner voice all along. From third grade at PMFS, through my senior year at GFS (both of which were Friends Schools of the Quaker background and philosophy), I had been a participant in weekly meetings for worship. This involved the whole school getting together in a meetinghouse and sitting still doing nothing. It was a form of meditation that I would get into even more as a martial artist. The whole idea beyond this meeting for worship was that we all have the light within. If at any time someone had a brilliant inspiration, it was believed to come from God. If such an inspiration arose, one was encouraged to stand up and break the silence by sharing the inspiration with others.

After all of my experiences in Judaism and

81

Catholicism, I realized that I blended in best with Quakerism. After all, there were no hard-set rules, no "You should do this" or "You should know that." Instead, we were encouraged to trust ourselves and the voice within. There is a little bit of God in each of us and I still believe that to this very day.

I might be a bit biased in my opinion for obvious reasons. In Judaism and Catholicism, I was never an equal; in the meditative silence of Quakerism, we're all one and the same. No spiritual rank and order, no straining to understand what's going on. Just a bunch of people sitting together in Oneness.

Obviously, the martial arts further reinforced the Quaker philosophy to which I had grown accustomed. I also realized that in the past, my inner voice had played a valuable role in my life, even before I knew it was there. Somehow, it had warned me against the perils of discrimination. Somehow, I had known it was wrong when my friend Sekou was treated unfairly because he was black. Somehow, I had known it was wrong when I heard anti-Semitic or anti-Catholic comments. If you allow it to do so, your inner voice can be a tremendous guide. I vowed from there-on that I would always trust my inner voice. It has never let me down.

Coming back to Earth and getting back to Tae Kwon Do, I eventually earned a black belt in the fall of 1990. At the time it was my most memorable achievement to date. It was one of the few things I had done entirely on my own. For just about everything else I had accomplished, someone else had been pushing me along. Tae Kwon Do was a path I chose to pursue alone, by my own volition. There were times I would come home, exhausted, with an assortment of strains and sprains. Occasionally family members would shake their heads, and wonder out loud why I was putting myself through all of this. But the martial arts had succeeded in teaching me a valuable lesson; I learned that when we bear down and put our minds to it, we can accomplish anything.

With all of the previous musings about religion and the martial arts, you might assume that by my early twenties I was well on my way to becoming the next Paramahansa Yogananda. Um, not so fast. Remember, we're talking about a naïve deaf kid who still had a lot of growing up to do. The words *girls, beach, keg party,* and *beer bong* still held a lot more appeal than, say, *it's time to start thinking about what you want to do with your life.* On top of that, I was still a fish out of water, a deaf person trying to blend in with hearing people. So of course, I would continue making more mistakes and questionable decisions, especially during the first few years as a hopelessly clueless college student.

Both academically and socially, I was on a roller coaster of uncertainty. At Temple University I found myself on academic probation one semester and pulled in a 3.34 GPA the next. I was an accounting major one year, a psych major the next. What in the world was I doing there? I had no idea. Social life was practically nonexistent. There were too many faces, all of them hearing. My best friends were my interpreters, Alyx and Mike. Without them, I would have flunked out due to academic incompetence or total boredom, whichever came first.

At home, I mostly hung out with the same group of friends I had played baseball with. At this point in time we were no longer the cute little ballplayers who won Little League, Pony League, and Summer Rec League championships. We were now bona fide party animals.

Hanging out with my buddies was always fun, especially before we turned twenty-one. Old enough to hang out but too young to hit the bars, we usually had to resort to sports for a good time. We would play baseball, basketball, touch football, and street hockey. When we were done with baseball, we joined organized softball leagues. We were forever young, at least until we hit twenty-one.

83

Once we were old enough to go to the clubs, something changed in the social dynamics. When we were immersed in sports, I could deal with not understanding everything people said. I was able to have enough fun shooting baskets or hitting home runs so that if I missed some conversational tidbits here and there, it didn't really bother me. But it was a completely different story when we started hitting the bars. Rather than passing a ball around, my friends were just standing there, beer in hand, hoping to meet some chicks. I still had a lot of fun hanging out with the guys, but it was harder to interact. I could talk to almost anyone one-on-one but immediately fell out of the loop whenever it expanded into a group conversation. It could be fun one moment and excruciatingly boring the next.

To get through the boring interludes, I would order more drinks. If I was hopelessly out of a conversation, back to the bar I went. While everyone was talking, I was drinking. After seven or so beers I would have a good buzz going. Then, suddenly I would re-emerge from the depths of isolation to once again become the life of the party. Whether it was giving someone a wedgie, telling X-rated jokes, or doing the old "pull my finger" routine, I had become an alcohol-driven animal. I may not have been a great conversationalist, but I could sure get everyone loose with rowdy, physical behavior. If you heard a whoopee cushion go off you could bet I wasn't too far from the scene of the crime.

During the summer months it would get especially crazy. I was practically swimming in beer. Every year, we would rent a house at the Jersey Shore and the antics would begin. Initially we rented at Wildwood, but eventually toned it down somewhat (for us) and got a nice place at the more laid-back Long Beach Island. Hanging out with everyone at the shore was much more enjoyable than going to the bars in the city; I knew everyone well, we had fun on the beach, and we partied hard together in our beach house. Of course, I was still lost in group conversations, but nonetheless managed to find a way to have fun.

Perhaps the best thing about it was that despite the occasional frustrations, I could still laugh at myself. Sometimes it was all I could do. One such incident that comes to mind occurred on the boardwalk in Wildwood:

On one hot, sunny afternoon, I had decided to go for a walk. It was a beautiful day and I loved "hitting the boards" where all the stores and arcades were. I took off by myself, leaving behind all of my friends who had yet to wake up and recover from the partying we did the night before. Ah, this was the life. The sun shined brightly as I strolled the boards and there was plenty of eye candy. Glittery gift shops on my left, the waves of the ocean gently rolling in on my right, and of course, hot women in bikinis. Rowf! In fact, many of these gorgeous babes were looking at me. I nonchalantly strutted by, basking in all the attention. Obviously, they must have admired my muscular body. *(Okay, so I had to suck in my gut a little bit, but so what?)* I grinned at the ladies. The fact that their eyes were still following me further inflated my adolescent, hormone-ravaged ego. Remember that scene in *Saturday Night Fever* where John Travolta strutted down the street to thumping disco music? Replace the leisure suit with Bermuda shorts and real groovy sunglasses, and that was me.

Soon, however, I got the feeling that something wasn't right. Another group of women stared at me as I walked by, but this time I noticed it wasn't the admiring glance my ego had deluded me into perceiving the first time around. Not only that, I immediately spotted a group of *guys* who were really giving me the eye.

Instinctively, I looked behind me. *Oh, lord.* There was a tramcar right on my heels, loaded with about fifty passengers. Not only was the driver beeping his horn and yelling at me to get out of the way, but I also learned that there was a loud, pre-recorded "Watch the tram car, please" blaring repeatedly over the speakers.

85

My face turned bright red and I felt like crawling under the boardwalk.

When I got back to the house I told the guys what happened and we all had a good laugh over it. What else could I do? For the rest of the summer, they would jokingly go to extremes to tackle me or push me out of the way whenever a tramcar was remotely in the vicinity. Sometimes, you just have to laugh. Laugh, and the world laughs with you. Sure, sometimes they're laughing *at* you, but you just have to smile and move on.

In between partying it up at the beach and my academic endeavors at Temple, I managed to continue my successful career as a supermarket clerk. My salary steadily rose over the four years I worked there (1984-1988) and I was given more responsibility. *Not bad for a deaf guy.* When I finished college—if that was even necessary— I could go full-time at the store and then settle down for life. Why not? I enjoyed the environment I was in, and most of the customers knew me well. Indeed, there were plenty of good memories.

One day, there was this psychotic woman who had lost all touch with reality in the store and she stripped naked, screaming all the while at the top of her lungs. She appeared to be about 300 pounds and her yelling could be heard throughout the whole building. Except for me, of course.

While everyone could hear her coming and quickly got out of the way, she rumbled straight toward the aisle where I worked. The entire crew from my department, thinking quickly, ran to my aisle. No, not to help. They wanted to *watch.* They knew this was going to be good.

The guys gathered at the end of the aisle and peeked around the end shelf. It must have taken them all the restraint in the world to not to laugh. Meanwhile, I was lost in thought as I quietly marked up boxes of cigars, blissfully oblivious to this naked version of Godzilla screaming in my face.

When I finally looked up and saw what stood before me, I did what must have been the double take of the century.

Eeeee-yaaaaahhh!

I must have jumped two feet in the air. I fumbled the cigars and dropped a few boxes on the floor.

Jesus Christ! What the...

Completely disoriented, I abandoned my post and stumbled out of there in a catatonic state of shock. The guys were laughing hysterically as it began to hit me that yes, there really was a large naked woman yelling at me. The police arrived shortly afterward and order was soon restored. Sure, the whole thing was over in a few minutes (actually, maybe a bit longer—I later heard that two police officers were arguing with each other because neither of them wanted to be the one who had to handcuff our oversized and underdressed friend). But believe me, the guys who were there that day will be talking about this for *years.*

Another exciting incident at the supermarket happened during the time I worked the night shift. Given how there were few people around the store in the wee hours of the morning, this shift could be excruciatingly boring at times. On one typically dull graveyard shift, I took a much-needed coffee break and noticed that a couple of other employees were behaving strangely. They were visibly shaken and one of them actually trembled as she sipped from her cup. You'd think that the place had just been robbed or something.

As it turned out, the place *had* been robbed. Cashiers, front-desk employees, and a customer or two were all lying on the floor while a pair of gunmen emptied the registers. Meanwhile, I was nonchalantly stocking shelves no more than two aisles away from all the mayhem. Had I just turned around the corner of the aisle, I would have been peeing myself instead of moping about how boring it was.

87

As exciting as it was to be working with nude women and masked gunmen, there was still the gnawing sense that something was missing. Whatever it was that was sorely lacking in my life, I didn't fully understand. Fortunately for me, there was a kind soul named Linda Baine who certainly had an answer.

Linda was the new Coordinator of Residence Education at the Pennsylvania School for the Deaf who ran the dormitory and the afterschool program. Sometime in December 1987, a dorm supervisor left his job and Linda needed to find a replacement over the Christmas break. She had ten days to find someone. By chance, she happened to be at a staff party where my mother was also in attendance. Somehow my name came up over the course of conversation and Linda suddenly remembered me from a time we had met briefly once before.

A few years ago, I had been asked by PSD to be a guest speaker on a panel involving deaf people with different educational backgrounds. A number of people were curious about what it was like for me when I was the only deaf student at GFS, so I showed up and answered some questions. As fate would have it, Linda was the interpreter at this event. Fast-forward to 1987, and here she was at this staff party, learning that I was still in the area and passing time as a supermarket clerk. She immediately figured out that I would be the perfect candidate for the job opening as Resident Advisor and afterschool program basketball/baseball coach. She knew that not only would the kids learn from me, but I would learn from them as well. I still had a poor deaf identity back then and Linda knew just what I needed.

Linda went out of her way to visit me at the supermarket and she convinced me that it was time to try something new. She pulled me aside as I was stocking the shelves and told me about the job opening at PSD, suggesting it would be a great opportunity in more ways than one. The job required supervising fourteen kids in a dorm, planning and running evening activities, and coordinating occasional off-campus trips. In addition to that, there would be the aforementioned coaching responsibilities for the afterschool program. I would coach sports from 2:30 to 4:00, then after that was done I would head to the dorm and work there until 11:00pm. The supermarket paid better, yes, but the deal with PSD included free room and board. I would get my own room on the boys' floor and be able to live there throughout the whole school year—even on weekends when the dorm kids went home. I could practically hear my party animal friends cheering wildly at the thought of me having my own place. *Toga! Toga! Toga!*

As much as this decision should have been a no-brainer, I struggled with it for a while. It represented a massive change in the comfortable, safe, boring life I led. Of the fourteen kids I would be responsible for, only a small number of them stayed in the dorm because they lived too far for daily transportation. The rest were in there because certain social workers had recommended such an arrangement; these kids had such difficult lives at home that it was agreed a dorm would offer a safer, accessible environment conducive to learning. This job was no piece of cake. It was going to be a big challenge and I knew it. On top of that, the supermarket still paid very good money. But then again, the supermarket wasn't providing me with a place of my own. *Toga! Toga! Toga . . .*

As I continued to wrestle with this decision, Linda could have easily hired someone else while I stalled in the face of the fast-approaching deadline. Instead, she actually came to see me two more times, to further explain why this job would not only be a great experience, but also an opportunity for tremendous personal growth. From a financial standpoint I was ready to turn her down, seeing how I was due for yet another raise in just a few months. Yet something gnawed at me inside and Linda did a great job of selling me on the virtues of PSD. Finally, with no more than a day or two left on the deadline, I called Linda and told her that I accepted.

Working at PSD was an entirely new experience. My entire existence prior to that involved being the only deaf guy at school, at work, or on the baseball field. Consequently, I was always out of the loop and had no choice but to follow what others were doing. Finally, it was time to stop being a follower and start being a leader. For the first time in my life, I had a considerable number of kids looking up to me for guidance. I didn't always have the answers, but Linda always had faith in me. Although she preferred to let me learn by doing, Linda gladly offered advice whenever I needed it. As with Deborah, my interpreter at GFS, I was once again under the wing of a hearing person teaching me how to be Deaf. At times it was hard for me to admit that a hearing person could be so much more fluent than I was at ASL (as was the case with both Deb and Linda), but I knew I was gaining valuable insight.

On one occasion Linda handed me a memo from the administration. It was an important announcement that needed to be shared with the kids in the dorm. Linda went over the memo with me and asked if I could explain everything to the kids myself.

"Oh, sure," I signed to her. "I'll run it by them, signing it over step by step. If the kids don't understand, I'll 'drop' my signing to ASL and repeat it."

"Whoa, wait a minute," Linda intervened. "You mean you will *adjust,* or *switch,* to ASL." I had signed "drop" as if ASL was one notch below the signed English I often used at the time. Linda clarified that ASL is not inferior—both English and ASL are legitimate languages in their own right. Most prelingually deaf kids respond to—and learn better from—ASL.

From that point on I made a conscious effort to improve my ASL skills as much as possible. Thus began the rebirth of a true Deaf (capital "D" emphasized) man. Or, as the saying goes in ASL, "True-business, Deaf". For me, the door to a new world had just opened.

Everything at PSD turned out to be one new learning experience after another. I soon discovered that during the morning and early afternoon hours, the recreation room of the dorm doubled as the playroom for an Early Intervention Program. As previously explained, deaf children of hearing parents are usually behind in overall linguistic and cognitive development due to lack of effective communication during their formative years; Early Intervention is where they work at closing the gap.

Again, from the ages of birth to five years there is a crucial window for children to pick up language. If sufficient communication has not occurred during these years, the child begins school having to play catch-up. This gap is a key reason why many deaf adults today can barely read at the fourth grade level. Some deaf people, like my parents, also blame the old oral schools—they insist that if they had received sign language instruction in their day, they could have learned so much more.

In the Early Intervention Program, I noticed that there was a comprehensive plan designed to facilitate the deaf child's social-emotional, intellectual, and linguistic development. Parents would come in with their deaf toddlers and drop them off in a play area where they got to interact with other deaf children. (In addition to this, PSD also offers home-based services.) They were supervised all the while by staff fluent in ASL who would lead fun activities designed to develop communication skills. Meanwhile, the parents would go upstairs and work with other PSD staff, who would educate them on ways to accelerate their children's development. Sign language classes are also offered, and this of course makes all the difference in the world.

Although I could understand the overall philosophy of the Early Intervention Program, its importance never really struck me until several years later, when a deaf couple I know began raising their three deaf children. My friends, George and Val Oshman, communicate with their kids exclusively through ASL. Their oldest child, Travis, completely won me over on the virtues of ASL when he was only four years of age. There are two incidents that stand out in particular, incidents that I always refer to when advocating on behalf of ASL for deaf children.

The first incident occurred when Travis' mom flew to Chicago to be with a relative who had fallen ill. Everyone at PSD was enamored when they saw four-year-old Travis, signing in fluent ASL, explaining to his teachers that his mom specifically flew to Chicago to help take care of the sick relative in question. His signing skills and ability to effectively communicate *exactly* what was happening (including the relevant who, what, when, where, and whys) was way advanced for a deaf child his age. In fact, he got in more details than what you'd expect from *any* four-year-old, deaf or hearing.

Most deaf children at that age, especially those who come from hearing families where there is no sign language communication, would have only been able to say something like, "Mom fly, gone", or just, "Mom gone", without the skills to elaborate any further. To see Travis saying, "Mom flew to Chicago because . . ." truly demonstrated the benefits of early exposure to ASL.

The second example with Travis is hilarious yet enlightening. One day, George and Val discovered that their dog had somehow escaped from the yard and was nowhere to be seen. In their endeavor to find the dog (which, fortunately, was successful), they made "Lost Dog" posters to distribute in their neighborhood. Four-year-old Travis accompanied Val as she stapled some of the posters on telephone poles.

Initially, Travis did not understand what was going on. He asked his mom why they were posting up pictures of their dog. In ASL, Val explained that if someone in the neighborhood saw the dog, they would recognize it from the posters and call their home. Travis indicated he understood how it worked and proceeded to help his mom put up some more posters. A few minutes later, they came across a telephone pole that had a poster of a man running for office. Travis tugged at his mom's shirt and pointed at the picture of the political candidate.

"Is his mom upset because he's lost, too?" Travis asked. Val cracked up and explained that the politician's poster was for an entirely different reason.

Granted, Travis had made a cute assumption with his four-year-old logic. It was amusing how he made the connection between the dog and the politician, but it was also significant in showing his level of cognitive development. His brain was clicking on all cylinders. He might have jumped to the wrong conclusion, but that was irrelevant. The important thing was, *he was thinking*. He was putting two and two together in the cute way that only a four-year-old can. He was fine-tuning his logic and reasoning skills. Had his parents not been able to communicate effectively with him from day one in a language that is fully accessible to him, he might not have even come close to the level of thinking and communicating where he is today. Instead of the painful *never mind* or *I'll tell you later* that many deaf children get from their parents, Travis got all of the input any growing child so rightfully deserves.

By taking note of Travis' experiences, you can see why PSD's Early Intervention Program (as well as numerous others throughout the country) advocates early exposure to language, particularly ASL. By encouraging use of ASL and an understanding of deafness, the Early Intervention Program helps parents close the communication gap with their deaf children so that they are better equipped to deal with their upcoming school years. Most important of all, it improves many parent-child relationships. What greater gift than to be able to communicate with your parents?

Pardon me if it appears I'm beginning to get a bit preachy about ASL. I admit that it's not as easy as I make it seem. I have also, through my observation and brief interaction with the Early Intervention Program, come to understand how hard it can be on parents to have to deal with deafness long before they ever get around to joining a sign language class. It is not easy at all. It's not as simple as, "Oh, you just need to take an ASL class and you'll be fine." It's a lot more complicated than that.

Several parents have more needs than just learning ASL; they often have a number of other difficult issues they must work through. Some, or all, may have lingering feelings of shock, denial, anger, and even guilt left over from the initial diagnosis of their child's deafness. One parent admitted feeling embarrassed when her child signed in public, and consequently felt guilty; did she not have a moral obligation to love her child unconditionally, instead of worrying about what others thought? Through the support of other parents in the program, she found that she was not alone in having those and many other thoughts and feelings. Consequently, she was able to deal with them better.

Conversely, through the Early Intervention Program, I found out that *I* was not alone, either. I only worked with the Early Intervention staff once or twice—when they asked me to share my own personal experiences with parents—but I learned so much from it. For the first time, I could see deafness through my hearing grandparents' eyes. I could never understand what the big deal was in the way they reacted (or over-reacted) to my deafness; when talking with parents in the Early Intervention Program, I finally got a sense of what my grandparents had gone through. I could finally understand their pain and difficulty in accepting my deafness.

One parent of a prelingually deaf child caught me using my voice (which is not perfect, but pretty comprehensible), and wanted to know nothing else but how her own child could develop his voice similarly. It was hard to explain to her that I had lost my hearing *after* acquiring speech skills, and that communication in ASL was probably more desirable for her child. Seeing the parents' initial denial, however, helped me better understand the denial I saw in my own family. Not only did I understand now, but also, I was able to accept it and even laugh about it.

In fact, shortly before I quit my supermarket job for good (I initially made an ill-advised attempt at moonlighting before switching solely to PSD), there was this one time that a relative came into the store. She approached Jim, a co-worker and good friend of mine, asking him where she could find me. The thing was, there were two people named Mark working at the time. Jim tried to clarify by asking, "Mark in the produce section, or the deaf Mark?" The relative in question gasped and gave him a shocked look. When she composed herself, she retorted:

"He's not deaf!" Jim scratched his head, backed off, and told her to wait a second. Then he came into the backroom where I was on break.

"Uh, Mark... " he began, "I have good news and bad news. The good news is, you're not deaf anymore. Congratulations. The bad news is, one of your relatives is out there. She's pissed!"

Rather than getting into a family argument I just took a deep breath, smiled, and went out there. I greeted the relative and laughed about it with Jim later on. Instead of being angry, I actually understood the denial behind the whole incident. It was nothing personal, no insult. I would just let the relative deal with it in whichever way she could. Later, when she was ready, she would come to accept my deafness and even make an effort to learn sign language.

Speaking of sign language, I must admit that however desirable, you can't just learn ASL overnight. It takes time and commitment. Some people have a lot of trouble when it comes to acquiring ASL; my grandfather, for example, was so uncoordinated in his signing skills that anytime he tried to sign the letter "D", he inadvertently wound up giving the finger.

Regardless of whether or not anyone is a natural at picking up sign language, it is certainly worth the

95

effort if you have deaf children. They deserve to be in an environment where they are comfortable and have access to all that is being said around them. Even if your signing skills are marginal at best, deaf children can, and do, become accustomed to your "accent" of signing, and are grateful that you have taken the effort to learn. Let me tell you, I can relate to this firsthand. When I started work at PSD, it felt so good to be able to relax and just soak up all the information that came through so clearly in sign language. It didn't matter if the signing came from native ASLers or new signers who struggled to find the right signs; the important thing was *access*, and for the first time in a long time, I had plenty.

Some parents of deaf children choose to take a different, more radical approach: Cochlear implants. This involves surgically implanting an electrode array in the cochlea and a receiver/stimulator in the vicinity of the mastoid bone behind the ear. When combined with an outer microphone that can be worn externally behind the ear, this system works as a bypass, carrying sound around damaged inner ear nerves that do not function properly. This is not a bona fide cure for deafness, however. There have been varying results and varying benefits (such as awareness of environmental sounds, some ability to recognize speech, and some improved speech reading), but there has never been a case of Joe Deaf going under the knife and coming out of it Joe Hearing. Although technology has been steadily improving, the cochlear implant is not exactly a miracle cure.

This is the part of the book where I would like to drop the subject like a hot potato and jump ahead to the next chapter. Let the cochlear implant advocates and opponents slug it out somewhere else—I have better things to do. But no, every time I do a guest speaking gig somewhere, there are always people who inevitably ask: *"So, Markie, how about that cochlear implant? You planning on getting one soon?"* Let's get this over with once and for all and address a topic I am no longer sure how to address.

When the first edition of *Deaf Again* came out in 1997 I trashed the cochlear implant. My reaction when the implant first came out was somewhere along the lines of, "They invented a *what?* They surgically implant it *where? Get that thing away from me!*"

With all due respect to those who have a cochlear implant or are close to someone who does, I am going to share why I reacted the way I did. I understand that there are many people out there with varying experiences and opinions about this sensitive topic so I won't claim to have all the answers. But one thing I can do is show you how the whole thing initially looked to a culturally Deaf person struggling to find balance in his life. Today, my attitude is more accepting now that I've had the opportunity to meet several people who actually like their implants—but just for fun, let's go back to the days when I vehemently opposed it.

After you've read this book from cover to cover, hopefully without falling asleep, you will notice the theme here is a Shakespearean one: "To thine own self be true." Let's face it; I failed as a hearing person. All of the attempts at fixing me did not work. It was frustrating and drove me up the wall. After all the trips to otolaryngologists, after being operated on four times to have tubes put in my ears, after being subjected to countless audiologist exams, after being fitted for hearing aids, after being forced to take speech therapy, after constant reminders to sit up front and read lips no matter how exhausting it was…, I'd had it. I'd absolutely had it.

Couldn't these people just leave me alone? Couldn't they stop poking around in my ears? Although I never really spoke up when I was younger, deep down inside I always wished that people would stop obsessing over my ears. I simply wanted them to appreciate *me*, the whole person. Couldn't they stop trying to fix me and just accept me for who I was? That was all I ever wanted.

Eventually that happened. Well, sort of. As you will see in upcoming chapters, the hearing folks in my family would soon come to terms with my Deaf identity. It was clearly obvious to them that in my case, hearing aids and speech therapy could not compete with what ASL and the Deaf community had to offer. As I found in my new environment at PSD, sign language gave me the opportunity to be one hundred percent receptive to all that was going on around me. No amount of speech therapy or medical intervention could ever come close to providing me with that kind of satisfaction.

Finally, even those with the most hardcore audist mentality backed off. It was a tremendous relief. Finally, I felt like I was free to be me—the genuine, true-business, deaf me. Until, that is, my family got wind of the cochlear implant. It was as if their audist ideals had crawled out from beneath the surface to antagonize me yet again. Once they heard about the implant, they were relentless. And all I could think was: *Make it go away!*

You can imagine my frustration when relatives tried to sell me onto the virtues of the cochlear implant. After all these years, they had finally let go of their pathological "fix it" philosophy—but thanks to this new gizmo, they were back.

They would bring it up in conversation. They would clip the latest magazine articles and mail them to me. They would utilize the worst weapon of them all, Jewish guilt. *("Don't you know how happy your grandmother would be if you could hear the birds singing?")* They were everywhere. It drove me nuts.

The worst argument came from a relative who said, "But Mark, you're so smart. You can *learn* how to hear." I sighed in exasperation. The implied correlation between intelligence and deafness left me scratching my head. Later on, I would learn that this is a common misconception; there are many who erroneously assume that deaf people who have residual hearing and speech ability are smarter than those who do not. With a similar

98

mindset, my own family apparently thought that it was my level of intelligence, not my degree of hearing loss, that made me a viable candidate for the cochlear implant.

Of course, I know that when they bug me about the cochlear implant, they do it out of love. They want me to hear because in their auditory-oriented world, the idea of life without sound must seem absolutely incomprehensible. Understandably, they want to reacquaint me with the world of sound.

But little do they understand that in my eyes, it seems like they simply cannot accept me for who I am. On more than one occasion we've argued about this to no avail. All we can do is respectfully agree to disagree. Hey, we're family; it's cool. In my other book, *Anything But Silent*, you can find all the gory details of one particularly crazy cochlear debate in the segment titled *The Impossible Ideal*. In a nutshell, I came out of it thinking that to some people in my family, it doesn't matter what I accomplish in life. To them, I will always be the guy who can't hear. Ouch!

With this experience in mind, of course I cringe when I hear about young children getting implanted before they're old enough to make an informed decision for themselves. (For those who truly want a cochlear implant, that's absolutely fine with me—to each his own.) I can't help but wonder if their families are consciously or subconsciously imposing auditory-based ideals onto them. I wonder if these children will grow up stuck in a world where they feel obligated to be something they are not. Kids naturally want to please their parents, but this is quite a lot to ask.

Further compounding the issue is the phenomenon we refer to as *plasticity*. As I mentioned before, it's been proven that the best window of opportunity for learning language is between birth and age five. When you see a four-year-old effortlessly learning how to speak Russian and French while a sixty-year-old is struggling just to read the directions on how to operate a can opener, you're witnessing two very different levels of plasticity right there. I'd like to take a moment to expound on this.

Apparently, the brain has an easier time establishing neural pathways that allow for quicker learning during the first few years of life. Research on this subject appears to indicate that as early as age three, plasticity begins to wane. So if a child hasn't had sufficient opportunity to learn language by age five, the odds are great that this child will be significantly delayed—in terms of language and other areas such as spelling and writing—for the rest of his or her life. (Note: Special thanks go to Dr. Jerel Barnhart for explaining this to me. You didn't think I went out and became a neuroscientist overnight, did you?)

What with our understanding of plasticity, it's no surprise that parents are rushing to get their deaf infants and toddlers implanted at earlier and earlier ages. They're taking advantage of a scientifically-proven window of opportunity. I totally understand the logic behind it. And it's behind the same logic where I will vouch for, over and over, the benefits of *sign language* for *all* babies, deaf and hearing, implanted or not.

So there you have it, my bona fide opinion: I'm more open-minded and accepting of the cochlear implant, but at the same time I'm chagrined when people think they need to shield their deaf children from sign language. Sign language is one hundred percent—repeat after me—*one hundred percent* accessible. If you're using sign language alone—and many parents of both deaf and hearing babies are doing so with remarkable success—then you have one hundred percent access to language. If you have children who are implanted, that's fine. You can use sign language in conjunction with that to fill in the gaps (and there *will* be gaps—no technology is one hundred percent effective). Bombard those neural pathways! Make the most of them while they're still there! That's all I have to say about it. I guess you could say that nowadays I'm more concerned about language acquisition than the cochlear implant itself.

Cochlear implants for babies and young children continues to be something people will argue passionately about for hours on end without coming to an agreement. If you watch the movie *Sound and Fury*, you'll see how the cochlear implant decision can split an entire family in half.

As for my opinion, the jury's still out. I work in a deaf school and I see more and more kids with the cochlear implant—yet they're still in a deaf school, and they're still deaf. It makes me think that with all the surgery, related risks, follow-up appointments, intensive auditory/speech training—all with no guarantee of success—maybe it's just not worth it.

Then again, I see several parents on Internet mailing lists who laud the success of their implanted children in mainstream programs. These are kids I haven't met, so who am I to determine whether or not the implant works? Furthermore, as mentioned before, I now work with several kids who have the implant. Some of them like it. Some of them hate it. Either way, I work with them—and their parents.

In the past, I've read about parents signing their kids up for the surgery and doing everything in their power to keep those kids as far away from the world of ASL and Deaf culture. Now *that* upset me. Nowadays, I'm seeing more parents of implanted kids learning ASL and encouraging their kids to make the most of everything they have—socializing with deaf friends, using ASL, and making the most of whatever benefits their implant offers them. This is more of a happy medium that I can live with. These parents are no longer looking at the implant as a magic cure-all. They're simply looking at it as another option that may or may not improve their child's hearing. They are also under pressure to make a difficult decision, spurred on by doctors and research which indicate the earlier a child is implanted, the better. Do I want to burn bridges with these folks? No. While I personally prefer that someone be old enough to decide for himself or herself before getting an implant, I'm not going to carry a political agenda against those who feel differently. I already know several deaf adults who have an implant and are powerful members of the Deaf community—it's great to have them with us. Do I want to alienate them? No.

You can see how I've struggled to come to grips with the cochlear implant. Keep in mind that I'm just one guy among hundreds of thousands who have vastly different opinions. If you really want to know if this thing works, I'd recommend you go out and interview a large number of people who have one. That's my philosophy: If you really want to understand deafness, ask deaf people; if you really want to understand cochlear implants, ask the deaf people who have them. Get to the root of the source. They'll be able to provide you with the real scoop.

For those of you who are still wondering if my opinion has changed enough to the point where I'd want a cochlear implant for myself: Nope, I still don't want one. I'm very comfortable with my Deaf identity, thank you very much. But this time around, I do advocate for more tolerance and understanding. Many hearing parents are getting their kids implanted, and many of those kids are someday going to join the Deaf community. It is our responsibility to welcome them. If we spend too much time criticizing their decisions instead of just educating them about the positive aspects of the Deaf community, we will push them away—and it will be our loss.

No, the Cochlear Corporation of America did not bribe me to soften my stance. What actually happened was I went out and had a few kids of my own (gory details to follow in an upcoming chapter). After becoming a father I noticed that every idiot and his brother was bombarding me with advice on how to raise my kids. And now I completely understand how hearing parents feel when deaf people like myself are too outspoken against their choices..., choices that are none of my business.

Okay, that's enough about the cochlear implant. Let's get back to PSD and move on. Obviously, getting a job at PSD was an incredibly positive experience. In the two years I worked there as Resident Advisor I slowly grew a strong sense of Deaf identity. Being with other deaf people and with hearing people who signed gave me an opportunity to be completely involved in a more enriching way than I ever had before. Rather than being an observer, I was usually an active participant. Other staff actually valued my input and opinions. Although I still needed to refine my signing skills somewhat, I felt like an equal amongst them. I also enjoyed working with the kids in the dorm—and it took me a while to get used to the fact that they actually looked up to me. Big deal, some people might say, as I was just a dorm counselor. But it was the first time I could recall anyone, anywhere, ever looking up to me. In all my years of succeeding in the tough academic environment at GFS, I had never once considered myself to be a leader, nor had I ever imagined that I held the potential to be one. At PSD, this was my first taste.

Although the kids looked up to me, deep down inside I looked up to them. Right before my very eyes they were developing social and leadership skills I'd never had when I was their age. Everyone interacted as an equal and it was reflected in their self-esteem and confidence; anytime a kid disagreed with something, he or she said so. Anytime a kid felt that something could be done better, he or she spoke up and offered another suggestion. When I was in school, I didn't dare rock the boat—I was too busy playing catch-up, too busy trying to fit in with hearing people. With my hearing family, with my hearing classmates, and in my relationship with a hearing girlfriend, I'd always felt I had to be super-nice and super-perfect to be accepted. There's nothing wrong with being a nice guy or trying to be the best you can be—but when you do so at the expense of your true inner feelings, it just doesn't work. It's called living a lie.

103

For example, earlier I mentioned that with my hearing girlfriend Karen, I would willingly go to movies with her and pretend to enjoy it because I didn't want her to feel bad. I wanted to be accepted—to be seen as a normal guy who could do anything with her. At PSD, on the other hand, I encountered students many years younger than I was who said, "Nah, I don't like to go to the movies. They're not captioned. I'd rather wait for the video to come out and then watch it captioned on my VCR." (And, a generation later, these same kids would successfully advocate on behalf of getting captions added in movie theaters so they could go out and enjoy a nice evening at the movies with their families!)

These kids were being *genuine*, living in the present moment and accepting fully who they were and what they felt. There was nothing wrong with being deaf, nothing wrong with waiting for captioned videos to come out. They knew it; I didn't. These kids were wise beyond their years and way ahead of me. Chronologically speaking, I may have been 22 years of age at that time. But the *real* me—the fully-actualized *Deaf* Mark Drolsbaugh—was only about one or two years old.

9

∷

One morning in March of 1988, I had myself a nice, vibrant workout at Tae Kwon Do class and then headed to work at PSD. It was a beautiful day and I felt particularly refreshed. Arriving early at PSD, I did some homework for a class I was taking at Temple University. I had a more balanced schedule, taking a few courses part-time and pulling in some As and Bs. This was much better than the time I'd had too much on my plate and wound up on academic probation, but college was still a somewhat hollow experience. In contrast to Tae Kwon Do and PSD, there was this sense of emptiness I felt at Temple, a gnawing feeling that I was missing out on something.

On this day, however, even a dreary homework assignment couldn't get me down. I finished quickly and bounced down the stairs of the dorm, ready for another day on the job. Linda was already in the hallway on the first floor and she greeted me with some unbelievable news.

"Did you hear about Gallaudet? The students are on strike." I did a double take. I must have misunderstood.

"What?" I asked. "The teachers went on strike? What for?"

"No, the *students* went on strike. There was an election for President of Gallaudet University and two of the three finalists were deaf. The hearing person won, and now the students have shut down the university and are demanding a deaf president." *Whoa!* This was something else. This was big; this was history. You could feel the surge in Deaf pride throughout the world. That whole week, March 6 to March 13, had everyone's attention.

Up until that point, I had never really given much thought to Gallaudet, which is located in Washington, D.C. Even though I'd heard about it, I'd never fully considered going there. Back in 1984 I had chosen Temple University so that I could stay in the Philadelphia area and be close to my girlfriend. Bad move, I know. But that was then and this was now, and now Gallaudet had my undivided attention. It had everyone's undivided attention. Students and staff at PSD posted banners in support of the Gallaudet students' quest (as did many deaf schools all over the world), and the whole Deaf community was abuzz.

It didn't take long for the events at Gallaudet to cause a stir in the hearing world, either. This protest—which came to be known as Deaf President Now—featured students, alumni, countless supporters, and many leaders of the Deaf community. Not only were the gates to Gallaudet effectively blockaded, but also there was an emotional march to the Capitol. At first there was local media coverage, but soon it went national. Greg Hlibok, one of the student leaders behind the protest, was interviewed on ABC's *Nightline* for the whole world to see. Jesse Jackson offered his support to the Deaf community. And so on, and so on. This thing was BIG!

The solidarity felt among the Deaf community was unbelievable. I could feel it in Philadelphia, and I knew there were deaf people who could feel it in Bora Bora. Dr. Elizabeth Zinser, the hearing President-elect of Gallaudet University, certainly felt it. She acknowledged what was happening around her and gracefully resigned her post.

Finally, on March 13, 1988, it was announced that Dr. I. King Jordan, a long-time deaf faculty member at Gallaudet, had been selected as the new President. The entire campus erupted in celebration, as did the Deaf community all over the world. For an in-depth, historical account of everything that led up to the Deaf President Now movement, I highly recommend Dr. Jack

Gannon's book, *The Week the World Heard Gallaudet*. As a Deaf individual, I consider this event to be one of the most significant parts of my heritage. Chalk this up as something to repeatedly tell the grandkids, with a deep sense of Deaf pride.

Shortly after the Deaf President Now movement, there would be some changes at PSD that would directly affect me. Sometime in the following year, it was decided that the dorm would have to close. The number of residential students had dwindled from fourteen to eight, a far cry from the days of residential life at the old PSD, which used to be located in nearby Mt. Airy. By 1983, the rubella surge of deaf students had significantly subsided, resulting in a predictable decline of incoming deaf students. On top of that, political interpretation of PL 94-142 and its proposed "Least Restrictive Environment" ideology resulted in a number of good students being pulled from PSD and placed into mainstream schools, whether they or their parents wanted it or not.

Today, many residential schools face similar issues. Instead of being ideal places for advanced education, several are becoming dumping grounds for deaf kids who couldn't succeed in the mainstream schools. By the time they finally transfer to deaf schools, they are way behind. My fear is that many people will look at deaf schools and surmise that they must be lacking, and perhaps make the same assumptions about the use of ASL in the classroom. I myself was once guilty of such an assumption. (We'll get to that part later.) The truth is, many deaf schools face the formidable challenge of having to fill up their classes with kids whom no one else could handle.

Getting back to the bottom line, it turned out that the decline in rubella babies and the advent of PL 94-142 had affected PSD's student population so much, that it was no longer economically feasible to run a K-12 school on what was a large campus. Given the political climate of the time and considering how many well-known deaf schools in the United States were closing, it would not be

107

far-fetched to presume that PSD could have been forced to shut down its entire program. But in 1984 PSD made the move to its current Germantown location, where it would no longer run a high school curriculum. Instead, PSD would offer an academic program for students ages 3-15, as well as Early Intervention services for ages 0-3. Since those big changes in the mid-eighties, PSD has bounced back quite strongly, becoming a big part of the Germantown community. (Note: During the 2001-02 school year, PSD continued its remarkable comeback by re-establishing its high school program.)

In 1989, however, the dorm closed down. Since there were only eight residential students left (out of about 175 students overall), it didn't make sense to have a residential program. Instead, it would be necessary to use the dorm building in such a manner that it could serve much more than just eight people. The dorm would close, and in its place would be the new Center for Community and Professional Services. CCPS would have a public relations office and a community outreach program which included sign language classes, adult literacy classes, social services for the Deaf community, an AIDS education program, and of course, a continuation of the successful Early Intervention Program. Closing the dorm was not a step backward, but instead, a step forward which made better use of the space available.

This step forward, however, meant that my days as a Resident Advisor were numbered. Of course, PSD was not going to kick me out on the street; Headmaster Joseph Fischgrund had seen to it that all residential staff were offered regular day jobs for the fall of 1989. For me, however, the changes in store presented a window of opportunity. It was either accept a job as a teacher's aide (the only position for which I was qualified), or transfer from Temple to Gallaudet University. Linda had often encouraged me to go there when the time was right—and at this juncture, the time was now.

In August of 1989, I did what I probably should have done years ago; I packed my bags and headed to Gallaudet University. For the first time in my life, I would be a student surrounded by deaf peers. What awaited was one of the most magical periods of my life.

During the two-week New Student Orientation program prior to the start of fall classes, I made a lot of friends immediately—something I'd never done in any other educational setting. In between getting to know each other and touring Washington D.C., there were placement exams and other stuff that would determine what level of classes we would be taking in certain subjects. Although NSO had many practical purposes, the best one was that it enabled us to establish a strong base of friends whom we could lean on for support for the rest of our college years.

Academically, I found myself totally out of whack. On the one hand, I kicked butt as far as English was concerned. The results of my NSO English evaluation test got me waived from general English requirements, so instead of two years of English (which students had to take upon the passing or waiving of a remedial English 50 course), I could take one year of Honors English and be done with it. But mathematically, I was a mess.

During the NSO math proficiency test, I bombed. I had no recollection of the complex formulas and applications I'd learned too many years ago. The best math work I ever did was at GFS in 1984 and at Temple in 1985. But in 1989, I couldn't remember squat. As a result I was required to take a remedial Algebra II class. I was incredulous. I wanted to give the admissions office a piece of my mind: "Excuse me, but I've *forgotten* more math than most of the incoming students will ever learn. Just write it up and give me my diploma already." Of course, it doesn't work that way. As far as Gallaudet was concerned, I was an English whiz and a math moron.

Shortly afterward, the admissions office informed me that several courses I had taken at Temple University, a total of thirty credits, were not offered at Gallaudet—so I couldn't get credit for them. I was dumbfounded. It was like a whole year's worth of work at Temple was tossed aside.

I started thinking that perhaps I'd made a mistake. *Let me get this straight: I have to take a remedial math class, and thirty credits just flew out the window.* This was definitely not a good start. All I wanted was a B.A. degree and it felt like I was going backwards. What next, were they going to shred my high school diploma and send me back to elementary school? As exciting as it was to be at Gallaudet, I'd had my goal firmly set in mind: To graduate as soon as possible. It suddenly dawned on me that if I'd stayed at Temple, I would have graduated much sooner. At this point I told my friends it was nice to meet them, but I'd messed around too much in my life and couldn't afford to waste any more time.

Fortunately, a friend I met during NSO, Vijay Advani, talked me out of leaving Gallaudet at the last minute. Yes, he acknowledged, there was some maddening red tape. Yes, he agreed, it was a setback. But no, he insisted, it would not be a waste of time. Instead it would be an opportunity. An opportunity to enrich myself, an opportunity to become someone I'd never been before.

Vijay pointed out all of the things I had missed out on as a mainstreamed student in high school and at Temple. There were plenty of positive experiences, both social and academic, that were waiting for me at Gallaudet. Wasn't NSO one of the most enjoyable times of my life? Couldn't I just taste the excitement of living in a different world, one that was one hundred percent accessible?

On top of that, Vijay added, my mainstream background had turned me into a mindless automaton. Whatever the hearing folks did, I followed—no questions asked. Now, I was in the Deaf world, my world. It was time to take charge.

"You've passively accepted everything that's ever happened to you," Vijay explained. "You didn't have a choice. You were alone in the hearing world, but it's not

110

like that here. At Gallaudet you can be anything you want. You can speak up for yourself. Now haul your butt over to the admissions office and get your credits back."

Vijay was right. I went straight to the admissions office and filed an appeal for further review of my transcript. Wonder of wonders, the folks in the office actually listened. I wound up getting fifteen of my credits back. For me, it was a great victory. It was nice to speak up for myself and get results. I realized that in the hearing world, I'd grown accustomed to the futility of it all. Namely, *sit down and shut up; wear your hearing aid; never mind, it's not important; I'll tell you later, just do what your teacher says.* Those days were over. I was now totally immersed in a world where I could speak up for myself. Even if my math sucked.

As fate would have it, my very first class as a Gallaudet student was that remedial Algebra II class I was so upset about. I arrived early for the eight a.m. class, grumbling how the quadratic formula has no relevance to my life whatsoever. My disgust, however, immediately switched to delight as the teacher walked in and introduced herself. She was a deaf woman, and she was signing in her native ASL. For me, this was history— my first ever deaf teacher. Unbelievable! Everywhere I looked, I could understand clearly what was being said, at the very moment it was being said.

Whenever the teacher or the students signed, information was there for me to instantly comprehend, as plain as day. With an interpreter in high school I was always just a little bit behind. By the time my interpreter would finish interpreting a question, the other students had already heard it and someone would inevitably respond before I had time to come up with an answer. Not anymore. Welcome to real-time education, baby! This was instant access, no more three-second delay. Finally, I felt like I was really *there*, experiencing everything as it happened. I wasn't living in a fishbowl anymore. I noticed

111

that I was incredibly relaxed, a big difference compared to how I was often on edge in high school. Wonder of wonders... was I actually *enjoying* a class?

Yes, I was. My teacher's ASL was too good to be true, it was blowing me away. Although I had passed my math courses at GFS and Temple, it took a lot of hard work and frustration at every level. For the first time anywhere, I was not struggling to grasp anything. The instructor's ASL was so smooth and clear that I could literally *see* the concepts and comprehend them right away. Her hands, utilizing the space around her, deftly gave the impression of factors dividing in the air. ASL, as I could see very well here, happens to be very spatial and conceptual, and I had much to benefit from this exposure. Yes, I'd had qualified interpreters in high school and college, but they weren't math teachers themselves. I'd had to follow them following spoken instructions, plus I had to glance back and forth between them and the blackboard. The bits and pieces that I missed were apparently more important than I'd realized. With the use of ASL, however, concepts were smacking me right in the face in a way that's hard to describe. I just couldn't miss.

As I was contemplating how my first exposure to ASL in the classroom was opening my eyes to an entirely new world, I couldn't help thinking of a book I'd once read, Alan Watts' *Cloud-Hidden, Whereabouts Unknown*. Watts was ruminating on the beauty of Chinese writing in 1970, when he said:

"I have always been in love with Chinese writing. Each character, or ideogram, is an abstract picture of some feature of the process of nature---that is, of the Tao, the Way or Course of the universe. When translated very literally into English, Chinese reads like a telegram. 'Tao can Tao not eternal Tao,' or 'Way can speak-about not eternal Way.' In contrast with English, and particularly German or Japanese, Chinese is the fastest and shortest way of saying things, both in speech and in writing. If, as seems possible, Mao Tse-Tung's people switch to

112

an alphabetic form of writing, they will be at a great disadvantage, for, as their own proverb says, 'One picture is worth a thousand words.'"

When I read this excerpt in Watts' book, I realized that he very well could have been describing the beauty of ASL; one sign is worth a thousand words. After my experiences with ASL at PSD, which then culminated at Gallaudet, I am one of the staunchest advocates for ASL in the classroom. It's a beautiful thing.

Not every teacher, however, was as fluent in ASL as the students might have liked. If I had to rank the teachers based on signing skill, I would use a scale that acknowledged levels such as beginner, intermediate, advanced, and native ASL. My estimate is that most of the teachers fall in between intermediate and advanced. A small number of them sign clumsily, and a small number are native signers. If you had a lousy-signing teacher, tough luck. If you had a deaf teacher who signed in fluent ASL, you hit the jackpot.

To me, however, a teacher's signing ability didn't really matter that much, so long as it wasn't horrendous. Yes, I preferred ASL, but it didn't bother me the least if I had a hearing teacher with a tendency to use SEE (Signed Exact English). SEE doesn't hold a candle to ASL in terms of convenience and practicality, but I could tolerate it. After all those years in hearing schools with no interpreter, *any* teacher who signed—no matter how awkwardly—was a blessing. Even if a teacher's signing skills were marginal at best, I still preferred that to having a skilled interpreter in a hearing school. With a teacher who signs, you can let your eyes wander; you can follow the teacher, glance to the students, and so on. With an interpreter, you have to just sit there with your eyes glued to that same limited space all day. It's exhausting on the eyes. Give me a signing teacher any day, even if she's using the Rochester method. The Gallaudet faculty, regardless of signing level, was an incredibly liberating thrill.

113

Despite my exuberance over the fact that all of my teachers signed, there were a number of students who complained about teachers who did not use bona fide ASL. Most of these students were prelingually deaf and native signers themselves. I was intrigued by their argument that every teacher should be using ASL because it wasn't that much of a big deal to me. Then I realized that I had an unfair advantage; my residual hearing was good enough so that I could use a combination of hearing and lip-reading, which was supported by whatever signing skills a teacher had. For example, I could hear a teacher's voice, but not comprehend everything she was saying; when she signed, however, that would fill in the blanks.

Likewise, if the same teacher signed something incorrectly, my ability to hear her voice and read her lips would compensate for the incorrect sign. Many prelingually deaf students do not have this ability. With this in mind, I decided to try an experiment. I would zero in on the teacher's hands, completely ignoring her voice and her lips. I was shocked to find that in many cases I became completely lost. It often looked like the teacher was signing in broken sentences. An inability to properly bridge two sentences could often make it look like the teacher jumped entirely off the point. It was disorienting. Later on, I would try this same experiment in a number of deaf residential schools, with the same results. Only when a teacher signed in true ASL was I able to fully comprehend what was being said. This led me to conclude that for prelingually deaf students, ASL is of utmost importance in the classroom.

Eventually, a student organization at Gallaudet took it upon themselves to publish an underground guidebook that rated the teachers based on their signing competence and overall content of classroom work. It was a brutally honest guidebook. The administration was not too pleased, and a number of teachers were livid. But it helped. I personally took advantage of it myself. When it came to taking courses that were related to my weakest areas, such as math and technology, I tried my best to make sure I got into a class where the teacher used ASL. Technical idiot that I am, I never would have received a B+ in the Television, Film, and Photography course if it weren't for the deaf teacher who signed in ASL. That's just the way it is.

As my first year at Gallaudet continued, there were more things I would learn about the dynamics of the Deaf world. Social life, not surprisingly, was incredible. I estimate that in about one or two semesters at Gallaudet, I'd made more friends than I ever had in an entire lifetime of attending hearing schools in Philadelphia. I was in Deaf heaven.

I also noticed that I was in the world's largest melting pot of deafness, and the wide continuum of deaf people with varying communication skills and backgrounds brought up some very intriguing issues. There are deaf children whose deaf parents are fluent in ASL and have a strong language base. There are deaf children whose hearing parents learn and use ASL. There are deaf children of hearing parents who use SEE, Signing Exact English, to communicate. There are deaf children whose hearing parents have no knowledge or interest in any kind of sign language whatsoever. There are deaf children whose hearing parents strictly enforced the oral method. Then there are those who are hard of hearing and late-deafened, some of them coming to Gallaudet with no sign language ability at all.

If that isn't diverse enough, now try to factor in the varying educational backgrounds of all of these deaf people. There are residential schools for the deaf, day schools for the deaf, mainstream programs in hearing schools, and then there are oral schools where signing is not encouraged. Some deaf children just attend hearing schools with or without an interpreter like I did, and find a way to get by.

Not only is the use (or non-use) of sign language an issue, but we also have to keep in mind the quality of the curricula itself. Some deaf programs are good, some are lacking. The same goes for mainstream programs. Some may be good in terms of academic content, but are insufficient nonetheless because of differing communication methodologies that leave some deaf students completely lost. Also, there are a considerable number of international students who come from countries where programs and services for the deaf are unheard of. And so on, and so on.

Now take all of these varying types of deaf people, with such diverse social and educational backgrounds, and throw them into the only university in the world for the deaf. What do you have? Several professors scratching their heads and wondering how to accommodate everyone.

Sometimes this presents an awkward situation. What happens is that some teachers in general requirement courses wind up lowering their standards to accommodate the deaf students who are significantly behind academically. Remember how I explained earlier that some deaf children are stuck having to play catch-up for the rest of their academic careers, due to lack of communication during their developmental years? This, alongside the fact that it's impossible for every high school in the world to have an excellent deaf program, results in Gallaudet professors having a number of students in their classes who can barely read a newspaper.

On the one hand, I don't like seeing classroom standards lowered for deaf students. But on the other hand, I completely understand this dilemma in which teachers of the deaf will often find themselves. It's not easy to teach a class where half of the students are potential engineers or CEOs and the other half can hardly read at the sixth grade level. Whereas hearing people can choose from many post-secondary institutions that best match their ability (be it a small junior college, large university, or perhaps Yale or Harvard), there is only one university for the deaf. Gallaudet professors have to deal with all of us, for better or for worse.

116

No, I'm not implying that Gallaudet is the *only* option for deaf college students. Many deaf people can and do attend hearing universities, some of which have programs for the deaf. Nonetheless, a wide range of deaf people with varying academic backgrounds choose to attend Gallaudet. It's a wonderfully unique experience, and it's hard to pass up.

Also, there's another dilemma for the teachers: Just because a student struggles with English—just because the front page of *The Washington Post* proves to be a formidable challenge—does not indicate that this student lacks intelligence. I've met several students who absolutely blew me away with their ability to argue, debate, and present intellectual concepts—in ASL, of course. I've met students who had trouble writing a coherent paragraph, yet they could easily program or repair a computer. (I, on the other hand, can write rather well but have much difficulty changing a light bulb.) It's a mind-boggling predicament.

During my years at Gallaudet—the early '90s—pretty much every deaf individual had a fair shot to succeed at Gallaudet. Sometimes, students with a stronger academic background were annoyed when teachers of general requirement courses modified homework assignments to accommodate those who were not as literate. No, Gallaudet is not a diploma mill; core courses related to your major, as well as most junior and senior year courses, were (and still are) appropriately challenging. It was usually just in a number of freshman/sophomore general requirement courses where teachers sometimes lowered their standards. It gave the academically challenged students an opportunity to make the adjustment to college. Some made it, some didn't.

Eventually, this changed somewhat. By the spring of 1995 there was an overhaul of some of Gallaudet's programs. Due to federally mandated budget cuts it was necessary for the university to come up with what was called the Vision Implementation Plan. Designed

117

for more cost-effective management of the university, the V.I.P. brought forth the elimination of some classes and programs that were deemed not challenging enough. There was also an innovative new program, called Literacy 2000, that was implemented to help students improve their English skills.

Based on these moves and also feedback from faculty and students, the bar for academic standards at Gallaudet was significantly raised, including admission standards. I know it could be argued that this might not be fair to some individuals who deserve a chance to catch up, but I feel that the responsibility was initially put in the wrong place. It is not Gallaudet's job to teach what should have been taught during grade school and high school. I feel strongly that it is the responsibility of early intervention programs, residential schools, mainstream programs, and junior colleges to effectively provide accessible education and services to prepare deaf students for the tremendous experience that is Gallaudet University.

After I got my general requirement courses out of the way, I really enjoyed getting deep into courses that were related to my psychology major. Outside of the classroom, I caught up on missed social opportunities of past years by making a good number of friends. Of course, quality is better than quantity, and I found myself mostly hanging out with one very special group. This group consisted of Jeff Jones, Vijay Advani, Jason McKinnie, Derek "Heavy D" Gambrell, and myself. You couldn't find a bunch of people anywhere with more differences than ours. Jeff and I are white, Jason and Derek are black, and Vijay hails from India. Jeff is from a Catholic family, I come from a Jewish family, Vijay is Hindu, and Jason and Derek come from different Protestant denominations.

It didn't matter. Living on the same floor in the Peet Hall dorm, we all became very close friends. We found that we all shared the same warped sense of humor and

118

bonded quickly. One Resident Assistant in Peet Hall noticed us hanging out and remarked that it was amazing how people who were so different could get along so well. Jason—who was my roommate—just smiled and said, "Hey... We're The Family."

I couldn't have said it any better. We really were a family. We really didn't care about our differences; above all, we were deaf first, everything else second. Our similarities in deafness overcame any differences in race or religion. In fact, we could share our experiences, both positive and negative, from our backgrounds. There was no right or wrong; there was no my-way-is-the-only-way righteousness that many supposedly religious people possess.

Often, usually on weekends, we would meet in room 206, where Vijay and Jeff were roommates. Unlike other dorm parties, however, ours were not always the wild, lampshade-on-the-head variety. Instead, we would stay up all night watching movies and having philosophical conversations until six in the morning.

The content of our discussions were so deep that Jeff and I have often discussed taking notes and writing a book about it. It was amazing. We were all so different, united only in deafness—yet by the end of a good discussion, we would realize that we were all one and the same—no matter if white, black, Hindu, Catholic, or Jew. If only everyone could learn how to appreciate this, what a better world this would be. There were countless times when one or all of us would come up with incredible philosophical insights, insights that came from within our hearts and the natural course of our conversation. We would come up with answers as to why there was fear, hate, prejudice, discrimination, and religious intolerance. We also came up with the solutions to those problems, all on our own. We felt that it was amazing how we could learn from each other and come up with such great concepts. We were, and still are, brothers. Our differences are at the surface level. Deep down at the core, we are all One.

119

We weren't the first, however, nor will we be the last to realize this. Anytime a group of insightful people get together to relax and shoot the breeze, sooner or later someone comes up with something that makes everyone say, "Whoa, that's *deep*." Far be it for me to imply that it was only our group which could do so. For all I know, my hearing friends might have had a group conversation going where they found the missing pieces to Einstein's Unified Field Theory. If they did, I must have missed it. With my deaf friends, I missed nothing. There are certain dynamics in the group process where we can learn so much from each other, but this is possible only if we have full, unrestricted access and input. Sure, I'd had interpreters at Temple University, but I couldn't take them with me to late-night discussions in the dorm. My education there was limited only to whatever happened in the classroom. At Gallaudet, the learning experience ran 24 hours a day, seven days a week.

In the spring of 1990 most of my friends took off for a wild spring break in Florida, but I stayed behind. An old friend of mine back home had told me he thought I had what it takes to play Division III baseball, even if it had been more than five years since I last threw a pitch. I figured I would give it a shot and tried out for the Gallaudet baseball team. I came, I saw, and I found out I couldn't pitch like I used to—but I made the team anyway as a shortstop. The experiences that would follow were amazing. They also served as a microcosm for everything I needed to learn about Deaf culture.

As I routinely attended baseball practice, there was another awakening of sorts. In academics, when I attended my first class at Gallaudet, it was like a huge relief. I remembered all of the stress I had gone through as the only deaf kid in high school, and finally I could now relax in a deaf classroom where I had unlimited access.

With baseball, however, I had *always* enjoyed the game, no matter who I had played with. Yet I began to realize that the Gallaudet baseball team brought forth yet another new world that I had never known existed. Whereas on past ball clubs I would just show up and play, the Gallaudet team provided an opportunity to be involved in everything, on and off the field.

Talent-wise, the best team I had ever played for had to be the 1984 GFS team, which won its league championship; I really had a blast playing with them. Because I was deaf, though, I was never involved in any of the locker-room banter or any of the pranks that went on. During road trips, I would stare contentedly out of the bus window while the others were joking around. I never really felt bad about it. I knew I was deaf, and that was just the way it was. I was just happy to get a chance to play. I didn't really know what I was missing anyway.

I didn't know what I was missing—that's what I now tell everyone who argues against my belief that deaf children should have the opportunity to interact with others like themselves. I have had many non-culturally deaf people tell me that they are doing great in the hearing world, getting by on oralism and never signing, and that they are happy and successful doing so. I, too, was once like that. I was proud of my status as the only deaf graduate of GFS; I was proud of my job at the supermarket; I was proud of my ability to interact with hearing people quite well. And *I just didn't know what I was missing.*

Being on the Gallaudet team more than woke me up to what I had been missing; I was experiencing baseball as I never had before. On hearing teams I just did my part and went home. Being on a deaf team meant nine players united as one. The communication I was part of on the field was entirely new to me. The catcher would sign some instructions to the pitcher, who would then advise me, the shortstop, to be on my toes for what might happen next. I would keep the chain of communication going by turning around and being sure the outfielders knew what was going on. Often, I would talk strategy with

121

the other infielders. The dialogue was continuous, a far cry from the days when I just stood there at whatever position I was supposed to cover.

Sometimes I would get a little weird, just to wake everyone up. Occasionally I'd give an outfielder a dirty joke in place of the usual strategic information I was supposed to relay, just to see if he was paying attention. I was able to be a leader or a clown, or whatever the situation called for. I never really got to be like this on any hearing team I'd ever played for.

The stories about Gallaudet baseball could easily go on and on for an entire chapter or more. One of my favorites is the time our coach, Vance, got tired of us forgetting our signals as he relayed them from the third base coach's box. He usually ran a complicated sequence of secret code signs which included decoys, the indicator, the primary signal, and signs that meant "try it again" or "ignore previous signal." It could get mind-boggling at times. On one occasion, a player on first base gave Vance a confused look as he tried to decipher an array of incoming signals. He was supposed to steal second base but he kept missing the sign. Vance sighed. Finally, he switched to signing in ASL, which the other team didn't understand anyway.

"Go ahead," he signed in exasperation, pointing at second base. "Steal second base whenever you want." The player did, and the team howled with laughter.

There was also Vance's favorite "dummy" play, where he'd have a runner on first base purposely drift too far off the bag. The other team would try to pick him off, and then he'd suddenly take off for second base. During the ensuing rundown, a runner on third would zoom home and score.

We would laugh about all of these antics on road trips, and we would swap stories and jokes on the bus. We told a lot of deaf jokes, we talked baseball, we talked about anything. I never knew that there was more to being on a baseball team than what happened between the foul lines.

I never knew that a baseball team could be such a close knit family. *I didn't know what I was missing.*

If the baseball team gave me a taste of leadership skills, that was just the tip of the iceberg. A number of my classes had group projects and presentations that required much teamwork and effort. Previously, I'd been accustomed to just going along with whatever my hearing peers decided to do. I was a puppet, the ultimate Yes Man with a hearing aid. At Gallaudet this was no longer the case. My input was not only expected, it was highly valued. It took me awhile to get used to this. I was so used to being left out of group situations that sometimes I would automatically zone out. My mind would just drift away whenever more than three people were discussing something. It was a natural habit that was born out of necessity—anytime my hearing peers or family got together, I could only manage to understand one-on-one conversations. On a good day, sometimes I managed two-on-one. But when a group got together, that was it. Game over. I'd be bored out of my mind and I'd always accepted it.

Again, back when I was a kid, it was ingrained in my mind that deafness was bad and *I* needed to be fixed—so if I couldn't understand anyone, it was my responsibility. Therefore I never complained when I was hopelessly lost in a group discussion. Instead of getting bored to tears, I just got into this habit where my mind would shut off from whatever was going on around me. It would entertain itself by flying off to some other world far, far away. Sure, I might have been cut off from the world around me, but at least I wasn't bored stiff. In a weird way this functioned as a screensaver for my mind. Why waste energy having my brain working when there was nothing I could contribute? For that reason, I often zoned out. I was a space cadet, and a frequent flyer at that.

With my deaf peers at Gallaudet, however, I had to unlearn this dissociative habit. I would be very talkative in small groups or individual conversations, but sometimes by sheer habit I'd space out in a large gathering of deaf people and find my mind fluttering all over the place. I would snap myself out of it by mentally reminding myself, *Hey, people are signing here. Come back to earth where you now have communication access.* Whenever this happened, I'd realize that five or ten minutes of conversation had passed and I had no recollection of it. Moonman Mark had done it again. It took me a while to break this habit because years of conditioning had taught me to react that way. As easily as Pavlov's dog started drooling, my mind could fly to another galaxy.

Fortunately, there were plenty of opportunities to shake this maddening habit. Hanging out with my best friends and playing baseball always kept my feet solidly grounded on this planet. Socially, I felt I was making good progress. Academically, I was always an excellent student individually, but I still needed work on group leadership skills. Group projects and presentations helped me to improve somewhat but I usually contributed just enough to accomplish what was necessary, nothing more.

In 1991, I came across some experiences that helped me get over the hump. I applied for a job as Student Resident Assistant in Krug Hall, a freshman dorm. As part of the Student Life program I was required to attend a number of professional growth workshops that demanded a high level of participation. It really introduced me to the dynamics involved in group and leadership situations, and I was expected to apply what I had learned to my job as much as possible. In terms of solving conflicts in the dorm or coordinating special events, this became easy enough once I got the hang of it. It was really nice to be able to do this. Finally, I got to understand what it meant to accept responsibility for a leadership role. In hearing schools, I'd never had the opportunity to be involved in anything like this. This was a good start.

The next step came shortly afterwards. I noticed that unlike in previous years, I faced challenges and confidently handled them. No more slinking off to hide in the library because I was afraid to face choir class. Gallaudet offered many challenges, in and out of the classroom, and I stared them in the eye. It was intoxicating. *Hey, I exist!* I began to *crave* challenges.

This led me to the Alpha Sigma Pi Fraternity, which I chose to join in the spring of 1992. Alpha Sigma Pi is a local fraternity that was founded in 1947; it was founded by and has always been run by deaf students at Gallaudet. This was the perfect fit for me as it represented everything I had gone through and had come to believe in. After being pushed for so many years by hearing family and teachers, I felt it was an ideal situation for me to join an organization which was run by the deaf, for the deaf.

While pledging for Alpha Sigma Pi I was required to work together with eleven other pledges. Sometimes it was hard but rewarding work, such as working in a soup kitchen. Sometimes it was silly work, going through the crazy rituals that fraternities are known for. Some of the supposedly weird things we did actually had cultural significance, especially in areas regarding Deaf history. That was part of the fun. Alpha Sigma Pi's emphasis on Deaf culture contributed a lot to our personal growth. It was educational, it was fun, and it was zany.

Whatever we did, it was a great experience because I learned so much more about leadership and running an organization. I had balked at joining any organizations at GFS or Temple University because I simply got left out. Besides, no one looked at me as an equal. I was always "The deaf guy". I would have been the loner staring out the window while everyone else discussed something. With Alpha Sigma Pi, I was on the same wavelength as everyone else. I was expected to be as fully involved as anyone, and I was. I wound up becoming an officer and served on the executive board as corresponding secretary.

Initially, I was in awe whenever the president asked me for advice from time to time. In the hearing world I'd been nothing but a bystander. I was not used to being involved in crucial decisions, some of which involved a considerable amount of money. I was not used to being asked to take risks and being responsible for them. These are skills you don't learn in the classroom, and they would come in handy in the real world after I left college.

There are some people who have responded negatively to my remarks about learning social and leadership skills at Gallaudet, arguing that college is not the kind of place where you spend thousands of dollars to socialize. While I was participating in an Internet chat group, such an argument surfaced. I was pleased to see that it didn't take long for another deaf person to jump in and point out that the lessons we learn outside the classroom are equally if not more important than the ones we learn inside. I can't emphasize this enough. We learn how to live life, the most important lesson of all.

Let's stop for a second and take a reality check. If you go back a few chapters in this book, you will recall how I had graduated from one of the best high schools in Philadelphia. The quality of education at GFS was unbelievable. However, when I went to Temple University, I had no confidence in myself. I felt awkward around the thousands of hearing faces, and it took me awhile to get settled down. I was shy and withdrawn, preferring to just go along with whatever it was that the hearing people around me were doing. I had a strong foundation of academic skills but had never put it to good use. When I got the supermarket job in my neighborhood I felt that was the end of the road for me: *"Not bad for a deaf guy."* I was like a car without a starter, parked in neutral, going nowhere. I had the tools but didn't know what to do with them.

Let's jump ahead to my senior year at Gallaudet and look at the difference being with my deaf peers made. I learned that I could influence other people and that I could be a leader; I learned how to make decisions, instead of blindly following others; most important of all,

126

I learned to set my goals higher. No more *"Not bad for a deaf guy."* I noticed many other deaf people at Gallaudet going on to successful careers, and having these role models around me meant a lot.

One such role model was not a fellow student, but a deaf teacher—Ms. Childs. She taught a psychology course I took during my senior year and she noticed I was coming down with a bad case of senioritis. I was a bit lazy with some assignments and had missed a few classes. Being concerned, she called me into her office for a meeting. Let's just say that it was a friendly reprimand, a small kick in the rear. Basically, her message was, "Never be satisfied; strive for more." If this advice had come from a hearing teacher, it might have gone over my head. I would have said, "Yeah, right, easy for you to say." But Ms. Childs was deaf, and she had a degree from Harvard. She was telling me I could do much better. There was no way I could ignore her message. From that day on I expected nothing but the best from myself. I was no longer going to sell myself short. Instead of perhaps going back to stocking shelves, I began to contemplate graduate school. A Bachelor's degree no longer appeared to be *not bad for a deaf guy.* I wanted more. I wanted a Master's degree, and then... who knows? My self-imposed glass ceiling was gone.

Granted, I began to expect more from myself in terms of academics and career possibilities. Socially, I had done the same; I was no longer the passive bystander. I had participated on the baseball team, joined a fraternity, and had the best group of friends a guy could ask for. Yet something was missing from the picture. I had yet to fall in love with a beautiful damsel, get married, have 2.5 kids and a dog, and live happily ever after. That was next on the agenda.

Before moving on to the sordid details of my love life at Gallaudet, let's conduct a brief review of my romantic endeavors in the hearing world. It will help you appreciate my (ahem) modest but meaningful relationships with the opposite sex at Gallaudet. In no particular order, here are some of the foul ups, bleeps, and blunders of my love life in the hearing world:

- A three-year relationship with Karen, which shouldn't have lasted more than a year. It dragged on for eternity because hey, she signed. I couldn't ask for more than that.
- A rendezvous with a very attractive hearing girl during a party at St. Joseph's University. I could not understand one word she said. After a few beers, I forgot I was deaf. We got along swimmingly for the next two hours or so, until I threw up on her shoes. End of story.
- A woman from my neighborhood who knew sign language jumped into a serious relationship with me. One problem: she still had another boyfriend. We were all confused and didn't know what we really wanted. It was very awkward. Hey, she signed. I couldn't let go, let alone realize how stupid this was. Big mistake.
- At a Temple University party, I had the very rare thrill of two women competing for my attention. One of them was the sweetest girl I had ever known. The other was a girl who signed fluently because she had a deaf brother. Unfortunately, this fluent signer also had a reputation for emotional instability. One guy specifically warned me not to get involved with her because "She'll bite you... She will really, really bite you." Of course, I go with the girl who signs. She tries to bite me, I flee the dorm at six in the morning, and I never show my face on that campus again.

There were a couple others, but by now you've pretty much caught on to the common thread: my choices were very limited. Of those examples, a *lot* of time passed in between. In fact, two years of absolute drought passed between my first dysfunctional relationship and the second one. I was often starved for love and looking for it in all the wrong places. Whenever an opportunity came, I would grab it, no matter how ill-advised.

During my years at Gallaudet, however, I learned a new word: Restraint. There were women everywhere, and they all signed. There would be no more settling for a woman just because I felt it was the best I could do. There would be no more clinging on to the rare ones who could sign, because at Gallaudet, *everyone* signed. And most of them didn't bite.

Lo and behold, I found plenty of opportunities for dating in my new environment. Wonder of wonders, I was actually being selective. If a certain woman didn't appeal to me, I didn't jump the gun. I had a few dates every now and then, but none of them turned into anything serious. I knew there would be others, and that I could wait for the right one to come along.

The right one came along in February 1991. Her name was Melanie McPhee and she was from British Columbia, Canada. Actually, she came along sometime in September 1990; I met her in the Peet Hall laundry room and was immediately smitten. Unfortunately, someone passed along a false rumor that she already had a boyfriend so I backed off. I had already seen what kind of disaster arises from dating someone who's already spoken for so I decided I wasn't going to make the same mistake twice.

But there was no other mystery man in Melanie's life, and she was going crazy trying to drop me hints that she felt a mutual attraction. I think she had to rap me on the head and say something like, "Kiss me, you fool!" before I got the idea. Either way, we officially had our first date on February 1st, 1991. I haven't stopped dating her since and she hasn't stopped rapping me on the head.

129

We built a unique relationship and became quite an item on campus. We were known affectionately as "Melonhead and Drolz" and were practically inseparable. Many people remarked that we appeared to be made for each other, usually because Mel seemed to be the only woman capable of putting up with my weird sense of humor.

Finally, the insanity came to a climax on April 18th, 1992. My Alpha Sigma Pi brothers were hosting their annual Cobrafest party, and we had a nice crowd of seven hundred people. One reason for the huge turnout, other than the live bands and the delicious bratwurst, was the eagerly awaited raffle. We'd sold a high number of raffle tickets featuring chances to win a computer, VCR, television, and a number of other valuable items. This was nothing new, since we do this every year. But this particular raffle was different—it was slightly rigged.

When the twentieth and supposedly final raffle number was drawn and the prize given to the lucky winner, everyone in the audience who didn't win began to shred their tickets and throw them into the air. Being one of the officers who was on stage picking out winning tickets from the raffle wheel, I began to frantically sign,

"Hold it! Hold it! It's not over yet!" The entire crowd stopped in its tracks.

"Due to the enormous success of our last party, Alpha Sigma Pi was able to add a twenty-first prize to this year's raffle." I held up a blank piece of paper and pretended to read from it.

"The winner of the additional mystery prize is... Melanie McPhee. Mel, come on up here." Melanie climbed on stage, and the crowd looked on curiously. Many of the people in the audience were aware that Melanie was my girlfriend. Either this was a fix, or something interesting was about to happen.

"Close your eyes, Mel," I began. "When I tap you on the shoulder, open them and see what the mystery prize is." She did as I told her. Immediately, two of my best friends, Tony Peeler and Jeff Jones, snuck up behind

Melanie and unfurled a banner. The crowd immediately began roaring. As I tapped Melanie on the shoulder, she opened her eyes and was initially disoriented upon seeing seven hundred people cheering wildly. Turning around, there was the banner:

Melanie, Will You Marry Me?

Right on cue, I pulled out an engagement ring and slipped it on her finger. Dumbfounded, Melanie began crying as her Delta Phi Epsilon sisters jumped on stage and swarmed us. Some people in the audience began signing, "Well? Well?" Oops. Mel quickly turned around and gave the crowd an emphatic "YES!!" All bedlam broke loose. Amidst the celebration, a teary Melanie grabbed me by the collar and signed discreetly: "I'm gonna kill you."

As special as that moment was, it wasn't over yet. We returned to Melanie's dorm room at two o'clock in the morning and she decided to call her mother back home in Fort St. John, British Columbia. With the three-hour time difference, it would only be eleven p.m. over there and this was certainly big news. Melanie went ahead and gleefully shared the events of the past few hours with her mother over the phone. After she hung up, I was so caught up in the moment that I figured what the heck, I might as well call up *my* mother. So I began dialing. Meanwhile, I forgot that my mother does not live in a different time zone. Up in Philadelphia it was two-thirty in the morning. What ensued was the closest I have ever seen anyone actually mumbling on a TDD:

"XCNMSSHERRY GA"

"HI MOM, BRAT HERE... GUESS WHAT? GA"

"HOLD... YOU WOKE ME UP   LET ME USE TTY DOWNSTAIRS HD

LKMDOKAY... GA"

"SORRY TO WAKE YOU UP BUT I HAVE GOOD NEWS... I JUST GOT ENGAGED TO MELANIE A FEW HOURS AGO GA"

131

"ARE YOU DRUNK QQ GA"

"NO IM SERIOUS WE GOT ENGAGED AT THE ASP PARTY GA"

"ARE YOU A FATHER QQ GA"

"NO NO   WAKE UPPPP!!! IM GETTING MARRIED CUZ I WANT TO... DUHHHH GA"

"OH WOW! CONGRATULATIONS   SORRY I AM SLEEPYHEADED WOW   WHAT A SURPRISE WONDERFUL... "

Thus began a new chapter in our lives. It was anything but ordinary, but I wouldn't have had it any other way.

10

::

After the wild events of the night I proposed to Melanie, I eagerly looked forward to getting married. I couldn't wait to make the jump from "I love you sweetheart" to "Take out the trash", and from "You look so sexy" to "You've got something yecchy in your eye." But it would have to wait just a little bit longer. Sure, I was about to graduate, but with a Bachelor's degree in psychology. In that field a B.A. means you're now qualified to work the fries section at the local burger joint. Melanie and I agreed that perhaps it would be best if I went after a Master's Degree before we tied the knot. This way I'd be more likely to land a good job, and thus would be more able to support us both when she eventually went after her Master's in Deaf Education.

In May of 1992, I walked across the stage in the Gallaudet Field House, shook President I. King Jordan's hand, and had my Bachelor's degree. It had taken eight years of bumbling around, but I finally had my degree. I'm not sure if anyone was more excited than my grandmother Rose, whose mantra over the past couple of years was, *"I wanna see you graduate before I die!"* My family shared the same joy and they got the unusual treat of seeing my two cousins, Trina and Daniel, also receiving their degrees that day.

For me, however, it was not really the same kind of celebration it was for my family. To them, it was the end of a long journey that had taken eight years. To me, it was just a stepping-stone, more of a beginning. I was looking ahead to grad school. I would be placed in Gallaudet's Department of Counseling as a School Counseling and Guidance major. So there was no teary goodbye to Gallaudet as I'd be hanging around for another two years. After having taken eight years to get my Bachelor's degree, two more years for a Master's degree wasn't asking for much. I was raring to go.

During the summer of 1992, my fiancée and I moved into a large apartment off-campus, rooming with another couple. We ended up running what looked like a kitty compound as we took in a stray cat that had three kittens outside. Soon, all four cats had made themselves at home in our apartment, and the females, those harlots, kept going out for a good time and coming home pregnant. At one point we had eleven cats coming and going. We were Bob Barker's worst nightmare. It took a "free kittens" advertisement and lots of Lysol to restore sanity to our place. (Yes, Bob, we screened the potential new owners and had our own cats spayed.) Melanie and I wound up keeping Shamu, a chubby black and white cat who resembles her namesake at Seaworld. Our roommates kept Sierra, Shamu's mother.

In-between frequent litter box changings, I found myself nervously anticipating graduate school. Was I ready? Did I have what it takes? I was nervous, but nonetheless looking forward to the challenge. I wanted to know if I could play in the big leagues. The fact that I had graduated from the undergraduate program Magna Cum Laude did not give me a sense that grad school would be a piece of cake. Yes, I'd learned a lot as an undergraduate, both in and out of the classroom. But there were no hearing students to compete with in the undergraduate program and some of my earlier courses had me wondering if maybe, just maybe, some teachers took it easy on me because I was deaf. I needed to find out if Gallaudet had prepared me sufficiently for the tougher challenges that would await me in graduate school—and later, for that big old hearing world out there. Turns out, it had. Graduate school was a struggle at first but I adjusted as I went along and wound up doing quite well. My teachers could be very demanding in terms of coursework, but very supportive in terms of supervision and mentoring. It was an environment that was *very* conducive to personal growth.

My only problem in graduate school came in the first semester when I had to seriously overhaul my study habits. In the undergrad program, it was possible to do homework at the last minute and cram all night for exams. It gives you time to do all the crazy things undergrads are supposed to do, such as attending pep rallies and swallowing goldfish. But graduate school is a full-time commitment and I learned this the hard way. It would take a figurative smack in the face to wake me up.

Using study and research skills that were still what one would expect to find at the undergraduate level, I compiled and handed in my first research paper. I was confident that it would rack in the "A" I had been so accustomed to getting. Oops, not so fast. It came back with an ugly "B-", and among the many red-ink comments was a scathing, "This is not a graduate-level paper." Cripes! I seethed, and then I came to my senses. No more cruising along with the coursework, I realized. It was time to put my nose to the grindstone.

From that point on, I pushed myself harder. I learned that the best way to succeed in grad school was to go one step further than the teachers asked you to. This meant using more references, putting in more effort, adding an angle which no one had ever thought of before, and so on. I had barely eked out a "B" for a couple of my classes during the first semester, but from then on it was hard work followed by excellent grades. I had learned my lesson.

One day, the daily grad school routine was stirred up a bit, when who else but my mother Sherry decided to visit. Somehow she wound up learning—and unlearning—a lot more than she or I ever expected. Sherry was in town for a workshop at Gallaudet that was related to her work at PSD. During her free time, she met with me for a shopping

135

spree in the Gallaudet bookstore. Soon afterward, it was time for me to go to my Psychosocial Aspects of Deafness class, which was taught by Dr. Allen Sussman.

I figured what the heck—why not invite Mom along? She was always involved in anything related to Deaf culture back home, so I figured she would get a kick out of this. This was the class where I was learning so much about deafness and family dynamics. It was often during this class where I would smack myself on the head and say, "Aha, so *that's* why so-and-so reacted to my deafness that way." It helped me learn more about myself and the people around me.

With Dr. Sussman's permission, Sherry sat in on one class. She would never be the same. Yes, she was in awe seeing a Deaf man with a Ph.D. teaching a graduate course. And the topic we covered that day knocked her out of her chair.

The topic was "Seven Attitude Dimensions As Measured By The Disability Factors Scale (Deafness)." Basically, we were reviewing certain attitudes and behaviors that are sometimes directed towards deaf people. There were seven listed on the handout and on this day we covered two of them: *Authoritarian Virtuousness* and *Imputed Functional Limitations*. The official definitions, quoted exactly as they appear in the handout are:

Authoritarian Virtuousness: This factor is distinguished by the over-favorability of the items. Despite the ostensible favorable tone of the content, it has a clearly unfavorable orientation. It pictures the able-bodied person as very warm and sympathetic toward deaf persons, advocates thoroughly favorable and preferential treatment of them, and ascribes special talents and personal traits to them, is full of sweeping and moralistic statements, and has a strong "do-gooder" flavor. It is, however, double-edged in that while endowing deaf persons with special qualities, it advocates tolerance for

136

their shortcomings. Further, it imputes inferior status to deaf persons, suggesting benevolent superiority on the part of the nondisabled person.

Imputed Functional Limitations: Focuses on the ability of the deaf person to function adequately and effectively in the environment, in specific occupations, driving cars, and general capacity in response to surroundings.

Shortly after we wrapped up our discussion on imputed functional limitations, my mother had one insight after the other. Her mind went back in time and suddenly, a lot of things made sense. It was like *Zen and the Art of Deaf Enlightenment.* As soon as class was over, she approached Dr. Sussman and thanked him for what was a very eye-opening lesson. She told him about her own experiences with imputed functional limitations, which Dr. Sussman would later ask me to share during the next class. The story that stood out the most involves Episcopal Hospital in Philadelphia, where I had an operation to have tubes put in my ears.

Sherry explained how one morning back in the early '70s, she had taken me to Episcopal for the surgical procedure. It just so happened that my hearing grandfather, Martin, worked in a printing shop not far from the hospital. He decided to drop in and offer his support before going off to work. He spoke to a few doctors briefly while Sherry signed me in, and then he tried to calm me down by assuring me that everything would be all right. I'd been through this operation before and I was obviously not too thrilled about going through it again. Once I was wheeled into the operating room, there was nothing more my grandfather could do so he left for work.

Meanwhile, Sherry waited..., and waited..., and waited. Two hours had passed, and no word on how the operation had gone. More time slowly ticked by. Three

137

hours after what was supposed to be a minor surgical procedure, there was still no word. Something was clearly wrong. At the other hospitals where I had gone through the same procedure, a doctor would come out and tell Sherry everything was fine as soon as the operation was over. On this occasion, however, a nurse kept peeking into the waiting room. She would make brief eye contact with Sherry and then quickly disappear behind the door.

Finally, Sherry reached the point where she couldn't take it anymore. She cornered the nurse to ask how I was doing. The nurse nervously insisted I was fine, and once again evaded any further contact.

Four hours after the operation—keep in mind I should have been out of there in thirty minutes—Sherry finally exploded the next time the nurse peeked into the waiting room.

"Where's my son?"

"He's in the recovery room. He's doing fine... "

"I want to see him," Sherry angrily demanded. "Now."

The nurse balked, but Sherry would have none of it. Reluctantly, the nurse gave my mom the standard hospital gown and cap required for visiting the recovery room. Extremely agitated, Sherry walked right into the room, and... found me surrounded by a bevy of beauties. I was wide awake, laughing and joking with three or four attractive nurses. I was passing the time by teaching them funny signs like, "The doctor is goofy."

Sherry was relieved, but she was also confused. What was this, Romper Room? Sherry wanted to go home, and I should have been discharged hours ago.

"Why can't we go home now?" she demanded.

"Uh, I can't really tell you," the nurse squirmed.

"Look, you said he's fine. I've been waiting for four hours, so you tell me *now* why I can't take him home." Sherry was positively steaming. The nurse stammered apologetically.

"I'm really sorry, but you can't take him," she said. "You're deaf."

I must have been only eight or so years old at the time, so a few decades have passed since this happened. But I cannot recall ever seeing my mother angrier than she was at that moment.

"WHAT? WHAT KIND OF IDIOTS ARE YOU? THAT'S MY SON IN THERE!" It suddenly dawned on her that the whole time the nurse was peeking into the waiting room, she was looking for my hearing grandfather. Yes, the *hearing* grandfather whom the hospital deemed the only person fit to take me home.

Absolutely seething, Sherry continued to argue with the medical staff. In the midst of all the confusion one of the nurses decided to call our family doctor for advice. Upon learning of the atrocity that was taking place, *he* exploded and gave the caller a tongue-lashing of his own. I was immediately discharged and sent home with my mother.

Dr. Sussman marveled at the story, shaking his head at the ignorance of the medical staff. As far as imputed functional limitations go, this one takes the cake. It's not that unusual to see people assuming that deaf people can't drive or hold good jobs. But here we had a case of medical professionals thinking that a deaf woman could not possibly be responsible for her own child.

Sherry had also remarked that years later, upon sharing that story, some of her friends would groan and tell her she should have sued the hospital. But after initially losing her cool, she just took a deep breath and let it go. She felt there was nothing she could do about it. It was just the way hearing people could be sometimes.

But at this moment in time, after observing Dr. Sussman's class, Sherry felt vindicated. A graduate class had just discussed, in great detail, the types of inappropriate attitudes and behaviors that she had been subjected to. On top of that, there were even fancy psychological terms for them. As Dr. Sussman later explained to the next class, "Now she has a peg to hang

139

her hat on." He was right. Sherry would never put up with discrimination from anyone again.

Over dinner that evening, Sherry and I would further discuss what we had learned in class. She pointed out that she could relate to many of the examples that were discussed. The same insight repeatedly popped up in our conversation: *"So that's why they treated us that way."* It was like someone had taken the blinders off and we could see social reality for what it was. We talked about some situations that had happened in the past, with a new understanding of how they related to the attitude dimensions covered in class.

It was an interesting trip down memory lane. Take, for example, the teacher in oral school who gushed, *"Oh, that's so wonderful!"* when Sherry barely managed to utter a sound. Never mind that the sound was incomprehensible and that the whole time this was going on, my mother and her class were far behind what would have been considered age-appropriate academic work.

Or, how about the airline attendant who'd actually held my hand and walked me to my seat when I told her I was deaf? That was mildly amusing, even if the other passengers looked at me as if I were a few sandwiches short of a picnic.

Then, there was the relative who smacked my mother's hand and admonished her for nearly wasting a quarter on a pack of gum when they stopped in a convenience store. He had his own brand of gum in the car and firmly ordered her not to buy the brand she preferred. Big deal, you might say, but Sherry was fifty-one-years-old when this happened.

Speaking of getting slapped, that's something that happened to her and many of her friends on a far more frequent basis when they'd attended the old oral schools back in their day. If they got caught using ASL, the one language they could clearly communicate with, they were sent to the principal's office for a nice little corporal visit. *Whap!*

140

The more we talked, the more the flashbacks returned. For Sherry, it was oral school and society's rejection of deafness in general. For me, it was several hearing people brainwashing me into believing that deafness was a curse that was to be avoided at all costs. It usually went something like this: *"Stop signing. It will ruin your speech. Wear your hearing aid. Raise your hand when you hear the beep. Can you read my lips? Oh, that's wonderful! You're just like any other normal hearing person. Don't socialize with other deaf people. They're isolated in their own inferior world and don't know how to succeed in the mainstream. It's a hearing world."*

It was flashbacks galore. It was amazing when we looked back and saw the attitudes and beliefs for what they were. It was absolutely incredible how after just one class, everything sort of clicked and just made sense. It was like we were finally validated, finally allowed to be who we really were.

The real kicker came from a separate handout, an article titled: *Deafness: An Existential Interpretation* by Stanley Krippner and Harry Easton.

One of the key excerpts:

If parents are not able to accept the fact that their child is deaf and continue to deny the implications of the deafness, the resulting effects on the child are to encourage his own denial and lack of authenticity. Such a child is thus unable to accept himself and his capacity to emerge or become a unique person is blocked. He lives an existential lie and becomes unable to relate to himself and to other deaf individuals and to the world in a genuine manner.

The above passage, in its simple beauty, explained *everything*. My frustrations and embarrassment, my unsuccessful struggle to fit in, trying too hard to please everyone, and my inability to "emerge", despite an excellent academic background.

As the evening wore on, the topic shifted from the attitude dimensions to the question of why we put up with them in the first place, especially in the examples

141

where we got it from our own family. For a considerable time, we had just accepted it. If relatives in our family ordered us around like children, if they expected us to stay for the duration of boring social events where we had no inkling of what was going on, we usually complied.

By the end of my senior year at Gallaudet, however, I had stopped being compliant. I had begun to assert myself and stand up for my rights as a deaf person. Just socializing with my deaf peers at Gallaudet had taught me that I deserved better than standing around with a phony smile. No, I would not alienate my hearing family and friends, I emphasized. At the same time, I would not subject myself to excruciatingly boring or uncomfortable situations, either.

If you go back a few chapters, you will recall that my social skills in the hearing world consisted of managing a few one-on-one conversations and smiling like an idiot whenever I was lost in a group situation. If all else failed, I would occasionally get drunk and forget I was deaf. Well, not anymore. Whenever my hearing friends got together and I was invited, I got into the habit of always bringing along at least one other deaf person. It could be Melanie, Vijay, Jeff, or my old pal from PSD, Michael Ralph. Sometimes it was all of them. Either way, I was not going to be the only deaf guy standing there wondering what was going on. If no other deaf people were able to join, I could still stop by and chat with my hearing friends for a brief time, and then leave when I'd had enough of trying to keep up with the conversation. Other times, if I just wasn't in the mood to do that, I would simply pass on the opportunity and not bother going at all.

The best thing about my new social philosophy was that I was no longer getting rip-roaring drunk. I would have one or two drinks, if any, and fully enjoy myself. No more Budweisers-for-boredom quick fixes; I was in control.

Normally, all of this shouldn't seem to be much of an issue. Surely, anyone could understand why a deaf guy wouldn't feel like staying too long in a room full of hearing people who don't sign. But for all of those years before I went to Gallaudet, that's exactly what I did. I put up with it, and always gave the impression that I was happy where I was. Before I had the support of my deaf peers, I'd always felt that I needed to look and act hearing in order to be accepted. So I would grin and bear it in a number of social situations where I wasn't really comfortable. I did this so much that my hearing friends and family got used to it.

Now, all of a sudden, I was putting limits on my social appearances. Everyone must have thought, *What is it with that guy? He goes off to college for a few years, and then comes back a total snob. He doesn't hang with us like he used to.* In fact, Dave, my best friend since little league baseball somewhat half-jokingly remarked to me,

"Hey, man, I thought you blew me off." Oh, far from it. That's the last thing I would want to do. I would never blow anyone off, but things were going to be a little bit different from now on. It would take time to adjust, but we did, like good friends always do.

As I continued to discuss all of these deaf/hearing social dynamics with my mother, I actually began to confront her. It seemed odd to me that Sherry was still putting up with awkward family social situations that I no longer tolerated. It was odd, because she'd always had deaf peers whom she could lean on for support; she'd grown up and gone to school with other deaf people. I, on the other hand, had been a hearing wannabe for many years, going to hearing schools and trying very hard to fit in with the hearing folks before finally attending Gallaudet. So why was I doing what was fair and reasonable, while my mother was tolerating hand slappings and the dreaded Dinner Table Syndrome with her hearing family? At age fifty-one, for heaven's sake, you'd think she'd say, "Enough already!" Why not, indeed?

The only explanation my mother could come up with was that her generation was so oppressed, they got used to being oppressed. Speaking up—uh, no, make that *signing* up—was never an option. As previously mentioned, her teachers had whacked anyone who dared to sign in class, as the oral method was strictly enforced. There were no prominent deaf role models to speak of, save for perhaps the relatively few "oral successes" whom most of the prelingually deaf could not emulate.

The lack of technology they experienced, as opposed to what we have today (TDDs, relay services, assistive devices, e-mail, text pagers, videophones, etc.), further contributed to my mother's deaf generation being overwhelmingly dependent on hearing people to help them. Yet the hearing did not know how to provide for the deaf what they really needed, so the vicious cycle of oppression continued—regardless of how well-meaning some educators and medical professionals might have been.

My generation, on the other hand, was the Deaf President Now generation. A generation that was able to assert itself and stand on its own two feet. So even though I'd joined my peers somewhat late, Sherry surmised, it didn't take long for me to assimilate their social values and opinions. In fact, it hadn't taken long for the DPN generation to have an impact on Sherry, either. Besides learning from my class and from talking about it with me, she had further conversations on similar issues with my good friends Vijay and Jeff. Impressed, she would go back home and tell her supervisor at work, Larry Brick (who is also deaf), what she had learned. His reaction was somewhere along the lines of, "Of course! Where have you been all these years?" He would assure her that it was alright to stand up for herself. Having gone through all of this, my mother suddenly realized that perhaps she had been *too* tolerant of a lot of things. She knew she had to make some adjustments.

Lesson number one would be how to handle the Dinner Table Syndrome, the phenomenon that occurs when there is a deaf person sitting at the dinner table with his or her hearing family. My father, Don, had been lucky enough not to have to deal with this until

144

he'd married Sherry. Since his own family was deaf and anyone could participate in dinner table conversation, there was no communication gap. After getting married, however, he found himself joining Sherry's family for dinner every now and then—and it was extremely frustrating for him not to be able to understand what was going on. He would eventually get tired of it and it reached the point where he would rarely attend any of their gatherings. He just couldn't tolerate it. Later, when I was older, the issue came up again. All Don would say about it was, "Someday, you will understand."

Someday was now. I decided to bring up the Passover Seder that Sherry had dutifully attended every year of her life. I had something like a twenty-five year streak of my own going, but by my senior year it was snapped. During my grad school years I didn't attend at all. I know, I know, that's awful. But I wasn't going to hop in the car, drive three hours up I-95, and then sit bored out of my mind for another three hours while my hearing family said and did things I could not understand.

My family chose to look at it as, "Mark can't make it because he has finals coming up," instead of, "He won't come up because the environment here isn't very accommodating for a deaf person." I told Sherry that if we really emphasized the *real* reason we weren't happy with the Seder, it could result in positive changes. We just needed to face the problem instead of hiding from it.

"But we've gone there for so many years," Sherry argued. "They're used to us sitting through the whole thing and not complaining. Also, they're getting old—it's too late for them to understand." But I disagreed.

"So," I began, "you'll have to just sit there for three hours, bored out of your mind. You'll really enjoy that?" Sherry shook her head no.

"So why put yourself through it? Why be the martyr? Work something out!"

I proposed simple solutions. Number one: If she wanted to stay for the whole duration of the Seder, simply hire an interpreter. Number two: If an interpreter was out of the question, just ask what time the Seder would start. If it was scheduled to start at six, simply show up at seven-thirty, which would be about the time dinner would be served. Enjoy the meal, say hello to the whole family, and just ask for permission to leave if the end-of-the-Seder prayers were too much to sit through. If anyone protested, *simply tell them the truth*: "I am deaf; it is hard for me to sit here and not understand anything."

Upon agreeing with me, but somehow wondering if I was going overboard with the deaf rebel routine, Sherry once again consulted with her boss and mentor, Larry Brick.

"Of course!" he responded. "If my family had a large event and they expected me to attend, I would bring an interpreter." He handed Sherry a copy of an old article he had written for a parent newsletter. It was about helping deaf children to cope with hearing family gatherings. Since he was deaf himself and knew how it felt to be left out, he never put any unfair social demands on his own deaf children. They worked out an agreement for family affairs: They would show up, say hi to the family, and politely join them for dinner. Once dinner was over and conversation began to drone on, the kids would discreetly excuse themselves. Then the kids would retreat to the TV or to the toys and magazines that they had brought along. Who could complain? It was common sense.

With all of this said and done, Sherry did something she had never done in her entire life: Prior to the next Passover Seder, she spoke up for herself in front of her family. For the first time ever, at age fifty-two, she actually asked my grandmother for permission to bring an interpreter.

Grandmom, however, felt uncomfortable with this and declined; it would have felt weird bringing in a total stranger for such a special family event, she implied. Sherry then countered with the argument that it was so hard for her to just sit there mindlessly while the whole family just talked and talked. Prayers were even worse; someone would try

146

to help by sticking a book in her face and pointing to the Hebrew that they were singing. This didn't help, because Sherry could neither sing nor read Hebrew.

At the mention of this, my grandmother seemed hurt. It was too painful for her to admit that her daughter and grandson were totally deaf. It was easier to think that everything was all right. So when my grandmother looked up she changed the subject and began talking about something way off the point. It was as if nothing had happened. My mother and I looked at each other in sadness; the denial we had just witnessed was very painful. Grandmom may have just switched subjects and gone about it as if nothing was ever said about our deafness, but we knew that deep down she was hurting. This was not going to be easy.

When Passover approached I was back in D.C., so I called Sherry on the phone and asked if she was going to go. She remarked that she had tried to talk about it one more time, and this time she'd actually made progress. Grandmom had finally, after all these years, admitted that she knew it was hard for us. She still wanted Sherry to show up for the whole duration, however. Her reasoning was that she needed help with setting up beforehand and washing dishes afterwards. I frowned. There are plenty of people who could do that. Why was it always my mom slaving in the kitchen while everyone else chatted over coffee? I argued with her that although she had made much progress in that they were now discussing the important issues at hand, the end result was the same. She was still going to show up for the whole shindig and would be bored to death. She admitted she really didn't want to, but... oh well.

On the day of the Seder, however, Sherry made history. She did not show up. She did what she felt was right—sort of. She called and said the dog was sick. When she informed me of this, I groaned.

"Oh, right," I said, "you didn't go because the dog was sick. Even the dog knows that's not the reason." Sherry laughed and admitted that was true. It was just easier to make an excuse.

"Well, the dog *has* been ill lately," I pointed out, "but what are you going to do when she's gone? What's next? You're not going to go because you're having a bad hair day?" Sherry laughed again and we joked about other possible excuses. It was turning into a David Letterman *Top Ten Reasons Not To Go To The Seder*. We made a bit of a joke out of it, yes, but it was really no laughing matter. For one thing, we felt bad because we knew that we kind of blew off the family. There just had to be some kind of compromise. Secondly, the dog thing just didn't cut it because only the truth, as we all know, can set us free. And finally, I realized I was pressuring Sherry too hard. She had made great strides; in fact, she would later be able to reach the reasonable type of compromise I'd been pushing for. At future family events, she would inform the family that she would be staying for just a little while if she was going to be the only deaf person present. If Melanie or I were there she would stay longer. It would work out great, and I was proud of mom; after fifty-two years, she had finally stood up for herself.

However, I also realized that I had been fighting my own battles with the family through my mother. Sooner or later, I would have to take a stand for myself as well. The time for that would come soon. I knew that if I wound up settling down in Philadelphia after finishing school, the same issues between my family and I would inevitably resurface. I knew I would handle it differently the next time around. After all those years at Gallaudet, I had changed. I needed to express myself and everything I believed in, instead of passively going along with what others had unrealistically expected from me. The Mark Drolsbaugh I really was and the Mark Drolsbaugh they wanted me to be were two entirely different people.

It was not going to be easy. Part of me was afraid that once I got out of school, seeing the real me might be too traumatic for my family. Whatever happened, I knew that I could no longer play the role of a fake hearing person anymore.

148

11

∷

During the second year of grad school things began to get a little crazy. In addition to the usual studies, I also had a wedding to prepare for and job opportunities to pursue. Somewhere in the middle of all that, I did an independent study project that took eight months to complete. It was a 175-page curriculum on health and wellness that I put together under the supervision of Dr. Frank Zieziula. He was interested in the concept of holistic wellbeing and its relationship to counseling, and as the resident health nut of the university I was thrilled to tackle this assignment. It also awakened a dormant love for writing. After a 175-page research project it dawned on me that *hey, I could write a book.* That's precisely what got me started on this very book you're holding in your hands right now.

The health and wellness study turned out to be a great release. I was able to throw myself into research topics such as exercise, nutrition, stress management, and meditation. Take my word for it; you need that stuff before a big wedding. This project, incidentally, was my last assignment of the year. Once completed, I had satisfied all of the requirements for a Master's degree.

Before we could move on from Gallaudet to the new challenges that were to come afterward, there was one more experience in grad school that sticks out in my mind. In the spring of 1993, my practicum assignment was to work as a school counselor trainee at three mainstream schools in Rockville, Maryland. It was my first exposure to mainstreaming. Previously, my only experiences in education involved being the only deaf kid in a hearing school, and also some exposure to a few deaf residential schools. Besides PSD, I had also seen and observed classes at both Kendall School and Model Secondary School for the Deaf, which are situated on Gallaudet's Kendall Green campus.

Prior to developing my counseling skills with individual students in mainstreaming programs, I was permitted to observe a few classes. It was interesting to be in the mainstream environment, of which the Deaf community has always had mixed feelings. Before I got to see for myself, the only things I had heard about mainstream programs were some less-than-favorable comments:

- They are socially restrictive by not offering social environments conducive to overall personal growth.
- Students have to deal with ignorance and discrimination from hearing staff and peers who don't know much—if anything—about Deaf culture.
- Due to the aforementioned limitations, students do not develop leadership skills, and this omission inevitably hurts them in the long run.
- Misinterpretation of PL 94-142 and subsequent legalities related to "Least Restrictive Environment" results in many excellent deaf students not being given a choice or a chance to attend good deaf schools. Consequently, the deaf schools lose valuable role models to mainstream programs and the overall quality of deaf education declines. In essence, many deaf schools become dumping grounds for kids who couldn't make it in the mainstream.

After everything I'd heard regarding mainstream programs, it was with much curiosity that I observed a few classes at Barnsley Elementary, Wood Middle School, and Rockville High School. Some students attended regular classes with an interpreter while others attended special classes that were for deaf students only. A small number of students had the option of doing both, depending on their individual needs.

The first class I got to observe was a group of twelve or thirteen-year-old deaf students at Wood Middle School. I was in for a surprise. They were going over their reading assignment which was a story from *Aesop's Fables*. I smiled, as I recalled how my late grandfather had also read those stories with me when I was younger. That's when the realization hit me: *Hey—these kids are actually reading material that they're supposed to read.*

I was dumbfounded. In my experiences with deaf residential schools, it was all too common to see many deaf students struggling to read material that was far below what would be considered age-appropriate. Yet these mainstreamed kids were reading the same material as their hearing peers. Inevitably, I began to question the quality of education in deaf residential schools. I recalled the time I wasn't permitted to transfer to a deaf high school as an eighth grader because I'd already exceeded the academic level of all the *seniors*, for god's sake. How could this be permitted to happen?

My wide-eyed observations continued at nearby Rockville High School, where I observed a group of deaf students discussing in-depth material related to the Civil War. Unbelievable, I thought. It was obvious that the mainstream programs in Rockville blew away any deaf school as far as academics were concerned.

Socially, the deaf kids did seem to be somewhat at a disadvantage compared to students at deaf residential schools—their interaction was limited mostly to socializing amongst each other as opposed to the overall (and much larger) student population. They didn't seem to do that much with other hearing students, although there was a rather large number of hearing kids taking an

151

ASL class at Rockville High. Regardless of the relatively limited social environment, this was still a heck of a lot better than being the *only* deaf kid in a school, as I had been at GFS. Granted, maybe there weren't as many opportunities where the kids could develop deeper social and leadership skills—and maybe there was always the gnawing feeling that perhaps they didn't measure up to the hearing kids, who were more likely to make the football team or become class president.

I struggled with this and other pros and cons. Perhaps any social ramifications were negligible as the kids could later catch up in an environment such as Gallaudet University or any local deaf club they could join as adults. Besides, if there were any social problems, that's what the counselors were there for. We often addressed a number of social issues and had counseling groups that would discuss adjusting to deafness in a hearing world. Most of the students, at least the ones I worked with, had a healthy and realistic attitude about their deafness.

By the end of my first week of working in the three mainstream schools, I vented out my frustrations about deaf education on my fiancée.

"Mel," I began, "for all of my years at Gallaudet, I've been pro-Deaf culture. You know how I didn't really learn anything about myself until I came to Gallaudet. You've seen me insist that the best classes for deaf kids are the ones in deaf schools where ASL is the language of choice. So why are the mainstream kids kicking their butts? Those kids at Rockville are so far ahead of deaf kids in residential schools—and their English skills are much, much better. What's wrong with residential schools?"

Melanie smiled and shook her head. It's nothing new when I get a bit too emotional and miss the fine print with my arguments. Melanie, on the other hand, has this knack for staying grounded. She also happened to be majoring in education, so she had the resources to answer my questions and concerns. She sighed and then

152

reached for an educational handout she had stored away in her files. She handed it to me and told me to read it very carefully.

I leafed through the handout and let out a long "Ooooooh!" It contained the findings of an extensive study which revealed that most *prelingually* deaf children tend to have the same reading and writing levels, regardless of whether they were in a residential or mainstream school. Oops. In the midst of all of the academic achievement going on in the mainstream schools, I had overlooked that factor. I realized that most of the students who had blown me away with their excellent reading and writing skills were in exactly the same boat that I was in many years before. Many of them had a significant amount of residual hearing and speech ability, which helped them pick up language during their crucial formative years. Thus they were not too far behind their hearing peers, if they were behind at all.

"But what about . . ." I mentioned a prelingually deaf student at Rockville who had also exhibited superior academic skill.

"Are her parents deaf?" Melanie asked. I smiled. Indeed, they were. Melanie then asked me to name a few prelingually deaf students at Gallaudet who had gone to residential schools and were from deaf families. I began to name a few. Among them was Kelby Brick, Larry's son—who'd graduated from MSSD, then Gallaudet, and had gone on to law school. In fact, *all* of the people I came up with were either in grad school or already holding good jobs. The dim light bulb in my head finally clicked on. It took a while, but Mel had effectively made her point. Upon taking a closer look I realized that there were some prelingually deaf kids in the mainstream program who did not come from families that used sign language. Predictably, they were significantly behind everyone else.

My conclusion? I cannot fully answer which is better, mainstreaming or residential schools. It depends entirely upon where you live. There are mainstream programs that have accessibility galore thanks to a high level of deaf awareness. There are mainstream programs that are totally ignorant and make you want to bang your head on the wall. There are deaf schools that leave you puzzled because you assumed their teachers would be well-versed in ASL—and they're not. Then there are deaf schools that are so powerful, so effective, that parents in the know will relocate—cross-country, if they have to—to enroll their deaf children at these schools. It's not easy, I know. But you have to really do your homework before enrolling your deaf kid in any school.

I can, however, once again identify the bottom line: The deaf child's access to language, or lack thereof, during the critical years from birth to age five. This responsibility ultimately falls upon the parents, not the school program. If a child is hard of hearing with significant hearing and speech ability, he or she may establish enough of a language base (and consequent cognitive development) to be close or equal to his or her hearing peers. If the child is prelingually deaf, it is very crucial that the he or she is consistently exposed to ASL for maximum access to language. The formula is simple: No language equals no learning. If there is neither language nor learning in the first five years of life, a child will spend the rest of his or her academic years at a significant disadvantage.

This is the reason why many prelingually deaf adults today can only read at the third or fourth grade level. I cannot emphasize this enough: If a child is prelingually deaf, exposure to ASL and the opportunity to use it is extremely important. Only the parents can see to it that this is accomplished. A more sobering fact: At a recent workshop, it was revealed that for virtually all children, 92 percent of learning occurs at home. There is only so much a school can do to bring a child up to par if it isn't happening at home.

12

∷

Duration the summer of 1994, Melanie and I flew up to her hometown of Fort St. John, British Columbia, for our wedding. Melanie's mother, Margaret, had already handled most of the dirty work by the time we arrived. She did a fantastic job of seeing to it that everything was taken care of and she made sure that all visitors, including my family, were comfortable and enjoying themselves.

Melanie's sister, Shawna, also did her share of work—and then some. In addition to assisting with all of the planning and coordinating, she graciously agreed to do a twelve-hour round trip drive to Edmonton where she would pick up my friends and groomsmen, Jeff Jones and Tony Peeler.

Shawna also had to deal with getting busted by the Canadian police. She drove a rental car was registered in my name only and, as Murphy's Law would have it, the police had a random check-stop on the highway. Shawna and her bemused passengers were stuck for hours in the middle of Canadian nowhere. It took quite a while to get out of that mess. Yes, Melanie and I had to drive down there and bail them out. It turned out to be a fun diversion from all of the wedding jitters, anyway. The movies *Road Trip* and *EuroTrip* were probably inspired by our misadventures. *CanadaTrip,* anyone?

By the time we got back to Fort St. John it was six in the morning, but it didn't dampen our spirits at all—we started our pre-wedding party right then and there. Other relatives and guests woke up surprised to find us indulging in all of the party food and beverages you'd

155

expect in the evening hours. A few of them even joined us, passing up the traditional bacon and eggs for pizza and beer. Hey Shawna, we love ya.

Meanwhile, Melanie's father, Bob, had also added some unique touches of his own for the wedding. Being a collector of antique automobiles, he prepped up two of them for the wedding procession: A 1964 Studebaker convertible and a 1965 Chevy Supersport. Melanie and I were going to get hitched in style, no doubt about it.

It was a great change of pace to be in Fort St. John after all of the craziness back in the States. Fort St. John happens to be on mile 42 of the Alaska Highway so you can hardly get any further away than that. Whether it was sitting out back enjoying the clear night sky and the Northern Lights, or relaxing indoors with Melanie's family, I was getting a much needed break from the hassles back home. I'm telling you; it's no surprise that we never see Canada in the news that much back in the States. We see so much coverage about war, disaster, and political struggles in other countries—but rarely do we hear about Canada, our quiet and friendly neighbor. They're too busy being real, genuine people up there. In Fort St. John people smile, say hello, and then leave their car running while they go into a convenience store to buy a newspaper. Try that in New York, eh?

On July 16th, Melanie and I had a beautiful wedding in St. Luke's United Church. At first I was nervous because some of my own relatives had expressed concern that the wedding was in a church. We actually took steps to make sure the minister wouldn't say anything that might be deemed offensive by those of a different faith. Looking back, I'm probably the moron who invented political correctness. See how out of control it is now? My fault.

Since I have absolutely no religious preference of my own, I wouldn't have cared if it was a Moonie wedding at the airport. But for a moment there, I was worried that someone might speak up during the infamous *If anyone should have any reason why these two should not be*

156

wed, speak now or forever hold your peace window of opportunity that always comes up at weddings. Who's the wise guy who came up with that idea in the first place? What kind of nitwit would actually want to introduce the idea of protest at a wedding? If you had any objections, wouldn't it make more sense to speak up *before* the wedding, thus saving everyone the hassle of planning, traveling, dressing up, buying gifts, and *then* having everything fall apart at the last second? I swear, whoever put that scary line in there prior to the "I do" must have been a drama queen.

Truth be told, I really was nervous because of the objections some of my family brought up due to their religious convictions. There were indeed some behind-the-scenes drama and we maneuvered through it as tactfully as we could. I'm not going to re-live it here. But if Melanie and I ever decide to renew our vows, my mind is made up: We're going to do it at the Elvis drive-through chapel in Las Vegas. I mean it.

Fortunately, and to the delight of everyone, the wedding was absolutely beautiful. The only suspense came from Melanie's seven-year-old nephew, Donovan, who wasn't too comfortable with the idea of being ringbearer. His quick-thinking mother bribed him with a Lego set and he kept his end of the deal. He performed his duties as ringbearer perfectly and was very patient during the long photo session afterward. I made a mental note that next time my family objected to anything I did, I would buy them a Lego set.

Seriously, the whole thing went perfectly, bordering on surreal. Melanie looked positively radiant and I was in a daze. As Melanie and I exchanged our vows, both families beamed with pride and joy. I kicked myself for worrying that my family would object enough to interrupt anything. Sure, we had our differences of opinion—but above all, we loved each other immensely. I noticed my grandmother, Rose, grinning from ear to ear. She was genuinely happy for me and had conducted herself with great dignity. She had, in fact, shown beyond a doubt that her love was unconditional. In the past I had, for whatever reason, felt that I always needed to win her approval, to be hearing, to be this, to be that. Today, she had effectively shown that she loved me no matter what. I had not only gained a wonderful wife, but also a more genuine love and respect for my family.

After the wedding and a great vacation in Vancouver, it was time to come back to Earth. Melanie and I returned to Maryland where a number of changes awaited us. There was, however, one particularly frustrating problem: I couldn't find a job anywhere.

During my time in Canada, I had looked into any possible school counseling positions, but there were none. Networking is everything, and in Canada I hadn't networked with anyone except the nice RCMP officers who almost seized my rental car.

Back east in Maryland I'd certainly made a name for myself—but so had thousands of other deaf people. Because of the close proximity to Gallaudet University there is no shortage of deaf people with advanced degrees in Maryland. The competition for jobs in Maryland's Deaf community is therefore extremely tough. In Pennsylvania, there were two openings but they were for a coordinator and a case manager at a mental health center. Not exactly what I had studied for, although I still threw my hat into the ring. Again, no luck.

Before I threw in the towel, there was an ironic twist of fate. A very good friend of mine, Michael Ralph, left his job as school psychologist at PSD to accept a similar position elsewhere. This meant that there was an opening in the Evaluation, Enrollment, and Counseling Center at PSD and it wasn't long before they contacted me. Although I'm a school counselor, not a school psychologist, PSD still decided to hire me. They had one other school psychologist and also another school counselor, but that counselor would be going on maternity leave the following year. Throughout all of this shuffling, they had decided to hire another school counselor, which turned out to be me. I would provide individual and group counseling services, crisis intervention, case management, and occasionally assist in procedures related to enrolling new students. Once again, PSD was going to play a major part in my life.

It was an eye-opening homecoming. Although there were a myriad of topics covered in both individual and group counseling, one thing that struck me quite hard was the prevalence of family issues, particularly those related to communication barriers. I realized right away that I've been very fortunate to have deaf parents and a deaf wife who understand firsthand what it means to be deaf. Most deaf children are the only deaf person in their family—and while I've had my share of frustrations with hearing relatives, there have always been deaf family members and friends with whom I could find a healthy balance. For deaf children who do not have this luxury, I had not realized how isolating this can be.

This soon became evident during the winter holiday season when PSD has a twelve-day break. While numerous staff and students had broad smiles on their faces as they eagerly anticipated their vacation, there was one young girl who caught my attention with an entirely different attitude. As fourteen-year-old Lori passed me in the hallway, I wished her a happy holiday and told her to enjoy the break.

"Oh, *boring!*" She shot back, "I don't want to stay home for twelve days!"

"Really?" I asked. "Aren't you glad to get a break from all the hard work you've done?"

"Yeah, but at home it's *boring!*"

"Why do you say that?"

"No one in my family can sign. Stupid family, boring!"

That explained it—I should have known. In the midst of all the holiday cheer, in my own excitement to escape

159

the blahs of the rat race, I'd completely forgotten that for some people the holidays can be quite frustrating. Lori was going to be twiddling her thumbs for twelve days.

I could not imagine how hard it must have been for her. Lucky me; I get to go home to my deaf wife and we can visit our deaf friends or our deaf relatives anytime. And as for the hearing relatives on my mother's side of the family, it's not that bad; there are usually more than two deaf people present who can keep each other company when that part of family has an event. Besides, should it get too boring, Melanie and I are grown adults who can get up and leave whenever we want. Lori, on the other hand, has none of the above, no such freedom. Asked to explain how that felt, she put her index finger between her lips and twiddled it up and down. *B-b-b-b-b-b-b-b.* That pretty much says it all.

After the break was over, Lori was thrilled to be back in school. So were a significant number of her classmates. I decided to ask them how their vacations had gone. Most of them said it was all right, as they shared stories of eating delicious food and getting new toys for Christmas.

Lori mentioned that she enjoyed the holiday food and gifts as well, but she also felt left out when she had to sit silently at the table as her hearing family chatted non-stop. I smiled and remarked that this was a common phenomenon known as the Dinner Table Syndrome. I asked the class how many of them had ever had to sit and just smile politely at a family gathering where they were oblivious to all the conversation going on around them. Every single hand in the classroom went up. Lori's eyes widened in surprise as she realized that her problem was not unusual for most deaf people.

"I sit there like a statue," said one student.

"I ask my mom what people say, but she says, 'Never mind,' or, 'It's not important,'" said another.

"My mom signs, but no one else in the family does."

160

"I can talk to my deaf brother, but that's it."

"I want to watch TV, but mom yells at me if I leave the table."

"I can lip-read, but only with one person at a time."

And so on, and so on. Every student had a story about how he or she tolerated the Dinner Table Syndrome. Lori was not alone. Now that we had all identified the problem, it was time to look for a solution. So what could we do? The class came up with the following possibilities:

- Encourage your family to learn sign language.
- Negotiate; tell your parents it's not fair to be expected to sit for an extended period of time with hearing people who don't sign. Get permission to excuse yourself so that you can go play a game, read a book, or watch TV.
- Invite a deaf friend or relative over, so you have someone to talk to.
- For really big, special events, ask for an interpreter.
- During a long vacation, arrange to visit deaf friends and classmates as much as possible.

These are all excellent ideas that I definitely support. As usual, the students had shown their insight and creativity in such a way that it was I who learned from them, instead of the other way around. They were absolutely right—with a little awareness and sensitivity, we can form a reasonable bridge between the deaf and hearing worlds. I knew I was going to enjoy working with them.

I also knew that I was working with the kind of staff that you get to collaborate with once in a lifetime. My immediate supervisor, Lisa Santomen Hellberg, has this remarkable therapeutic gift of being able to get other people to see themselves in a different light. One of my rookie mistakes as a counselor at PSD was to try to fix everything for everyone; Lisa taught me to instead guide the kids in such a manner that they could figure out for their own game plan to reach their goals.

Lisa also highly values the team approach and thanks to her philosophy, we've had the opportunity to collaborate with some very gifted professionals. One of them, Sam Scott, is a dynamic family counselor who adds new meaning to the phrase, "Think outside the box."

Sam is the kind of counselor who will get right to the root of the issue through the most creative strategies. For example, there was this one time Sam intentionally got into an argument with me in front of two eternally bickering students; as we yammered back and forth, we had the two students' undivided attention. Then, at the drop of a hat, we abruptly got up and left. The two students actually followed us out the door to see if we were okay. Together. They weren't arguing anymore. They got along fine the rest of that day. As some other staff wondered just what in the world Sam was doing (and it worked!), Sam calmly replied: *They had our attention. It was our job to get their attention.* This is the kind of guy I really enjoy working with.

There have also been situations that went far beyond the scope of a school counselor's ability. It's an unfortunate reality that when deaf students face significant mental health issues such as childhood trauma, maladjusted behavior, sexual and physical abuse, and other issues of a more clinical nature, it's difficult to obtain accessible mental health services in a quick, timely manner.

There are also situations where a particular student probably shouldn't be enrolled at a regular deaf school due to significant clinical issues, but there just isn't any other place they can go. They're considered deaf first, everything else second. I'm not saying this is right or wrong. It just is. On the one hand, it gets overwhelming at times. On the other hand, we've had success stories that you absolutely wouldn't believe if you didn't see for yourself. And these are success stories with kids that no one else could handle.

(I don't think the outside world gives PSD enough credit for this. Just my honest opinion.)

When I first started working at PSD, it was not uncommon for counselors to refer out the tougher clinical cases only to have them bounce right back. There simply weren't any mental health agencies that could provide a signing therapist or a competent interpreter. The Americans with Disabilities Act was still in its early stages and it was a slow, gradual process before things got better. During this challenging time Lisa made sure we had top-notch clinical therapists such as Cass Levin-Spause, Dr. Annie Steinberg, and Dr. Jeff Naser available for supervision and support. I cannot tell you enough how much it meant to us to have these professionals working with us, and mentoring us, until mental health services for the deaf in Philadelphia became accessible enough for us to refer out our most challenging cases.

Thanks to the improved access in our community we've been able to focus on more guidance counseling-related topics such as social skills, problem-solving skills, study skills, sex education, drug/alcohol awareness, and preparing for the future (be it applying to college or finding a vocation). Services are now more streamlined and *every* student at PSD gets access to a counselor offering proactive guidance, as opposed to the old model where a small number of clinical cases took up most of the counselors' time.

I also feel compelled to add that the restoration of the high school program had a tremendous impact. I can't imagine all of the politics and red tape that Headmaster Joe Fischgrund had to maneuver through in order to make this happen. I've heard rumors that he faced opposition when he did this but I don't have any juicy details. I'm just glad he got it done. You can see the difference in the students' attitudes all the way from preschool and up.

After the high school was reinstated, there were of course some growing pains—but once everything was in place, and especially after the first high school graduation at the Germantown campus, all of the students seemed to gain a greater sense of purpose. Seeing PSD students going through the college admission process, finding jobs through the World of Work program, and then graduating and coming back to visit with a ton of stories—whew, it had an incredible ripple effect. It's not unusual for a middle school student to approach me and ask how a student who graduated two or three years ago is doing ("He's still at Gallaudet? Great!"). When younger students can see the end result of the work they're being asked to do now, they take it more seriously. I'm so glad the high school is back.

13

::

When I returned to PSD in 1994, my wife and I got a modem for our computer. Thus began yet another adventure. Through our America Online account we began to explore the vast expanse of the Internet world. To our delight, there were newsgroups and mailing lists that covered deafness-related issues in depth. We found deaf and hearing people from all walks of life sharing their perspectives. Remember that Deaf Chat Syndrome I mentioned earlier? It's gone online.

I adopted the online persona of "Deffman" and had a lot of fun sharing my views with a worldwide audience. Little did I know, naïve Internet newbie that I was, that my opinions wouldn't necessarily be welcomed by everyone. I initially stated my opinion that ASL and interaction with deaf peers is *The Answer* for all deaf children. I beamed contentedly, knowing my deaf wisdom would change the world.

It didn't. Granted, there were many positive responses, but I also got flamed to bits—by other deaf people. A number of them were oralists who had no interest at all in ASL and the capital-D Deaf culture as we know it. Some of them were deaf people who signed, but nonetheless considered themselves "hearing-impaired" and chose not to be actively involved in the Deaf community.

I was dumbfounded at first but soon realized that the deaf population throughout the world was more diverse than I'd ever imagined. I'd thought that I had the answers for everyone, but soon found that what was a thrill for me might be a bitter pill for someone else. Despite the very real frustration of oral failures that I've described in this book, there *are* oralists out there who have succeeded at what they do. They're perfectly happy the way they are and have done very well for themselves in situations that were unbearable for me.

One such oralist pointed out that if I preached my way as the answer for *all* deaf children, I was just as bad as the old-school teachers who had forbidden the use of sign language in their classrooms. Who was I to say my way was the only way? He had a good point. With that in mind, I took the notes of what eventually became the rough draft of this book and changed everything to an autobiographical format. Instead of a general book on deafness, I've chosen the safer route of sharing my own personal experiences. You are, of course, free to draw your own conclusions and I encourage you to do so. If this book stirs just one healthy debate somewhere, I've done my job.

One day, I received an e-mail from a woman who was tired of the same old oralist vs. ASL arguments that were all too common online. She pointed out that many of the debates focused on oralists who preferred to be a part of the hearing world, and the culturally Deaf who advocated involvement in the deaf world. Very nice, she said—but what about those who are stuck in between? What about those who don't quite fit into the hearing world, and who also don't fit in with the deaf world? In other words, what about those who are "on the fence"?

She had me there. I hadn't really given it much thought because over the years, I'd pretty much immersed myself in the deaf world. Nonetheless, there was a time when I was still in limbo, floating somewhere between deaf and hearing. I remembered how I had wanted to attend PSD during my high school years but had to stay at GFS. I remembered how initially, when I first got involved in the Deaf community, my signing skills were somewhat awkward. In fact, many deaf people at both PSD and Gallaudet had remarked that I appeared to be *hearing-minded*—my signing ability and mannerisms were closer to what you would expect from a hearing person.

It didn't matter. I plugged on. Based on past experience, I knew that I would never completely fit into the hearing world. Period. That's it, that's a hardcore fact that will never change. Sure, it's possible to assimilate into the hearing world with varying degrees of success depending on residual hearing, speech, and lip-reading skills, but you can never fit in completely one hundred percent.

However, any deaf person, given a reasonable amount of time, can sufficiently learn how to use sign language; I did. And gradually I became a part of the deaf world in a way I never could have with the hearing world. To this day, I have never seen a deaf person learn how to hear and use that ability perfectly in the hearing world, yet I know of countless deaf people who have found success and happiness in the deaf world after years of struggling in the hearing world.

Granted, there are those who remain on the fence and simply don't feel a bond (or a need to bond) with the deaf world. This is understandable. For example, during all those years at GFS, English and English alone was my primary language. ASL, as we all know, is a completely different language with a completely different syntax. So if you're joining the deaf world late, it can be very frustrating because you are literally joining another culture—and it's nothing unusual to experience culture shock.

On many occasions in the deaf world, I would sign (in English word order) a hearing idiom and be greeted with blank stares. Conversely, someone might throw me an ASL idiom, a sign or signed phrase that had no English equivalent, and I'd be confused. It took awhile to adjust, and I can see why those who are on the fence might feel like they're in a completely different world. They are.

Is there any solution to this uncomfortable limbo of not quite fitting in here and not quite fitting in there? That depends on individual preference. As for me, I had two solutions that helped me adjust to the deaf world.

Number one: Find others who are going through the same thing you are. In other words, the best way for people on the fence to find comfort is to find other people who are on the fence. During my early years as an employee at PSD, as a student at Gallaudet, and as a member of a deaf club, I found other deaf and hard of hearing people who were also relatively new to the scene. We had a lot in common and we were able to give each other a lot of support. In due time, we all became more culturally Deaf. I'm eternally grateful for the experience.

Number two: Find a mentor in the Deaf community. It helps to have a special friend who is culturally Deaf, yet sensitive to your needs as a 'New Deafie'. In my case, it was my friend Vijay who at the very last minute talked me out of leaving Gallaudet University in 1989. As mentioned earlier, there was some frustration at the beginning that made me question whether or not I was in the right place. I might have given up on it were it not for Vijay. I might not be writing this book if it weren't for him.

Of course, I realize that my solutions do not apply to everyone. I'm simply telling you what worked for me. It still needs to be acknowledged that there are a lot of people who just don't feel comfortable in Deaf culture, and no one should force it on them. The only recommendation I can offer that works for everyone is this: Find your peers, whoever they may be. If you consider yourself hard of hearing, if you don't really like signing that much, keep in mind that there are many deaf people who feel the same way; find them. The worst thing about being on the fence, in my opinion, is the feeling that you are alone. Whoever you are and whatever you believe in, you can find your answers.

If you were to ask me what my own personal approach to deafness is, I'm going to go all philosophical on you: *Be at one with your deafness*. This coincides with a concept found in Tai Chi, another martial art I became involved with after moving back to Pennsylvania. One of the principles of Tai Chi is the fact that it is usually not recommended to go directly against an opponent's force; instead, it is best to go *with* the energy, using an opponent's own force against him. When someone tries to push you, don't resist head-on. Simply yield and turn in the direction you are being pushed. With just a little nudge, you can send your opponent flying off in that direction with the very energy he was trying to use on you.

In applying this principle to deafness, I found that it is similarly foolhardy for me to directly resist it. Just be deaf, I learned. Struggling against deafness and trying to be hearing (something I'll never be) goes against the flow and it is incredibly exhausting. Why fight it? Rather than trying to fix myself into being the person that other people wish I could be, I have found that things have worked best when I just focus on my positives and take it from there. I make the most of what I do have, instead of wasting time on what I don't have.

For some people, such a philosophy is incomprehensible. One such person wrote an article about this which appeared in a Philadelphia newspaper. I found it quite perplexing. The author in question could not understand, in any way whatsoever, why so many deaf people were saying no to the cochlear implant. She could not understand why some of us don't want to be fixed. After all, she mused, the deaf must be missing out terribly on wonderful sounds such as birds singing, ocean waves crashing on the shore, and the wonders of music. In addition to that, this woman couldn't understand why deaf people value sign language so much. She argued that sign language, for all its richness, has serious drawbacks. It's not possible to 'talk' in the dark, with your back to someone, or with your hands full, she surmised.

169

Although her concern was well intentioned, it nonetheless overlooked the fact that what might be important to hearing people may not necessarily be important to the deaf. Instead of listening to Luciano Pavarotti with our ears, we can watch awe-inspiring Deaf Poet/Storyteller Peter Cook with our eyes. Although there are deaf people out there who can and do enjoy music (either through residual hearing or by feeling the vibrations), it's not that big a deal. Truth is, there are *several* ways to find spiritual enjoyment. For some, it may be hiking through a nature area. For others, it could be mountain climbing, reading a great book, painting, or many other examples. For me, walking at night along a moonlit beach is inspiring. Do you see me writing an article claiming that people in Kansas are spiritually deprived because they don't live anywhere near a beach? Of course not. There are countless wonders in this world, and countless ways to enjoy them.

As for the comments about sign language drawbacks, it needs to be pointed out that everything has advantages and disadvantages. Sure, I can't sign in the dark, but how about those loud nightclubs and other places where hearing people have to shout into each other's ears? Deaf people in such noisy environments can sign to each other conveniently, without any problem, and even across the room if necessary.

As for not being able to sign with your hands full: Is there anything more disgusting than verbally talking with your *mouth* full? Give me a break. Pure and simple, different people have different abilities. Let us enjoy what we can, and don't worry about what we can't. I feel that we're better off celebrating our differences instead of imposing our values onto each other.

Basically, I recognize that no two deaf people are alike and that each person has a right to their individuality. If you're deaf, and if you're comfortable being deaf the way that only *you* can be deaf, then more power to you. Whether you consider yourself capital-D Deaf or hard of hearing, that's something only you can decide for yourself. Personally, I believe our diversity is fascinating and there's nothing wrong with being different.

For example, I can enjoy music, and I can recognize certain songs by certain artists. I can even learn the words to some of those songs. However, I can't speak with hearing people on the phone by voice, no matter how hard I try. (I need to use the TDD or videophone relay services, like most deaf people.) Meanwhile, my old roommate Jeff is the exact opposite. As far as music goes, he can't recognize any songs by any particular artists. Yet somehow, he can speak on the phone by voice with his hearing relatives. Hey, it's an ability he has, good for him. It was interesting to see these differences in each other, differences which were so pronounced that we would jokingly accuse each other of being hearing. Regardless, we both consider each other culturally Deaf.

So, is there a specific look we're supposed to have, a specific way we're supposed to act? I don't think so. We all have the right to be individuals. If a deaf person accuses me of brownnosing with hearing people when I use my voice (yes, it has happened), I shrug it off. I'm only taking advantage of an ability I have. What's wrong with using it? On the other hand, if someone tries promoting exclusive oralism for prelingually deaf children, I often speak up for the virtues of sign language. I have done so many times in debates that have raged online, with varying levels of support and disagreement from other participants.

So what's the answer, really? The closest thing I could find came from one of the more levelheaded members of a particular Internet mailing list. After much haggling over this communication philosophy and that communication philosophy, this education style and that education style, a great guy named Chris deHahn mercifully intervened with a classic posting. With his permission, I offer you his original note as it came out in April 1995:

171

The cure for deafness is our deaf children.

Sometimes I think we spend so much time theorizing, studying, working toward our methodologies that we forget why we're doing it and who we're doing it for. It doesn't matter what methodology we choose. What matters is that we teach our children to be open minded and objective. We need to focus on their abilities, instead of their disability. If a child is a beautiful signer, we need to praise him or her. If a child has beautiful speech, we need to praise him or her. If a student does well in class, we need to praise him or her. We must teach our children tolerance of others' beliefs. We do this best by example.

Tolerance and understanding are the best lessons we can teach our children. It's so much more important than sign language linguistics or proper oral pronunciation.

There is a cure for deafness. We can cure it by showing the world our children and their accomplishments. We can show the world a world of deaf children that can communicate differently, yet they all respect each other for their differences. We can show our politicians, our business leaders, our community leaders, that our children are different yet they are capable of anything. Our children will break down the barriers of deafness. We owe them our patience, our respect, and our help.

Amen, Chris, Amen. This is the closest I have ever seen anyone come to a solution to deafness that applies to everyone. When parents and professionals look for the magic answer for deafness, they invariably wind up arguing over communication methodologies. Even though ASL has been a godsend for me, I can't preach it for everyone. However, if people are willing to put aside their strong opinions about this communication method or that communication method, I do believe I have a general formula which guarantees success

172

for most deaf children. It is quite simple, really. Deaf children need:

1) Loving, supportive parents
2) A communication system which is effective for them
3) A good school with full accessibility
4) Consistent parental involvement at school and at home
5) Successful deaf role models
6) High expectations—from both parents and teachers
7) Lots of reading and writing
8) More reading and writing
9) Repeat 7, 8, and 9 as necessary

If it looks like I've put considerable emphasis on the parents, well... exactly! For virtually all kids, deaf or hearing, it has almost always been parental support that has allowed them to conquer the many challenges they face while growing up. Simply being involved, providing a loving environment, and encouraging achievement is almost always enough. My own parents, and especially my grandparents, didn't always know the answers to dealing with a deaf child, but they were always there. In the long run, that was more than enough.

Before we move on, there's one more topic related to the aforementioned formula for success. Something happened in 1999 that absolutely blew me away and made me realize that in order for all of the tips and suggestions to really work, there must be a crucial ingredient sprinkled over all of them: Unconditional positive regard.

It was at a Family Learning Vacation at the Governor Baxter School for the Deaf (located in beautiful Mackworth Island, Maine) where I was asked to run a couple of workshops for parents of deaf and hard of hearing children. This wasn't specifically for parents of GBSD students; it was for families all over the region.

In addition to working with the parents, I was also asked to talk to a group of children. Most of them were hard of hearing and between the ages of ten and thirteen. At first I wasn't sure exactly what to do with this group, but ultimately I decided to open the floor and have a rap session. I wanted to see what these kids would say behind closed doors, away from the parents and teachers for whom they'd been on their best behavior. What followed was a candid discussion I'll never forget.

There was this one kid, about twelve years old, who stood out entirely. The topic of our discussion was how we, as deaf and hard of hearing individuals, handled large family events. More specifically, what do we do when totally lost in a room full of chattering, hearing relatives?

This one kid, the twelve year old, said, "I say 'Hello'— and then run!"

I asked him what he meant by "run."

He explained that he would approach his relatives on a one-by-one basis, engage in some superficial conversation, and then he'd make a hasty retreat before the conversation evolved beyond "How are you," "How's the family," and "How's school." Unbeknownst to virtually everyone, this kid was manipulating each and every conversation.

He was an expert at lipreading superficial conversation because he knew what to look for. But he also knew that if anyone changed the subject, he would have been like a deer frozen in the path of oncoming headlights. So he took control, mastered the art of how-do-ya-do, and moved on as quickly as possible.

"Isn't that exhausting?" I asked.

"Yeah," he admitted, with several other hard of hearing kids nodding their heads affirmatively. "Sometimes, I sneak out and go to my room to play Nintendo for a while."

It was not just the young boy's confession that struck me hard—it was also the knowing looks on the other kids' faces. This twelve-year-old kid had validated the experiences and frustrations of everyone else in the room that day.

I was so moved by what transpired that I've included excerpts of the above anecdote in articles posted on the Internet, as well as in two other books (*Anything But Silent* and *On the Fence: The Hidden World of the Hard of Hearing*). I've often been contacted by deaf and hard of hearing people who told me they were in *tears* when they read it ("Oh my god! That's me!").

One thing I try my best to explain to the world at large is: Some of us wear hearings aids. That's fine. But some of us also wear hearing *masks*. We feel compelled to look and act hearing because we think that's what everyone wants. And that brings us back to unconditional positive regard. It's absolutely crucial. If you have deaf and hard of hearing kids and you don't want them growing up to be nut cases, they need to know it's okay to be deaf or hard of hearing.

Whatever the degree of deafness, and whatever methodology (or technology) is used in conjunction with it, it's very important that kids have a sense that they are just fine exactly the way they are. The technology and other stuff, they need to understand, is nothing more than a tool that may or may not help them get by. Either way, they are fine just the way they are. I can't repeat this enough.

14

::

Eventually, Melanie and I found a nice townhouse in North Wales, Pennsylvania. Melanie earned her Master's degree in Deaf Education and wound up becoming a fantastic teacher. And then, we received a tremendous triple blessing. On January 21, 1999, Darren Michael Drolsbaugh was born. Brandon Reed Drolsbaugh followed on December 13, 2001. And finally, Lacey Marissa Drolsbaugh joined the family on June 27, 2005.

It is here where things have come full circle in an incredibly positive way. Whereas this book opened with my own birth—a veritable horror story—Darren, Brandon and Lacey arrived in the age of accessibility. For all three kids, we had everything. TDDs, interpreters, and even captioned TV. The interpreters, especially, were a tremendous help while Melanie went through labor, childbirth, and follow-up medical care. Melanie and I had not bothered with any of the Lamaze classes that many couples take, figuring it was all hooey anyway. (We knew that at the first hint of pain, Melanie was going to scream for an epidural.)

Nonetheless, when a kid is ready to plop out of your wife, nurses give specific breathing instructions, instructions that help immensely. These are instructions that would have gone completely over our heads without an interpreter. It was an absolute godsend and we welcomed our kids into the world with much joy.

Compare the birth of our kids to my own birth in 1966 when my parents were left in the dark, and you can see how we've come a long way. And of course, above all, the most important thing is that we've been blessed with a wonderful new family.

Inevitably, people wind up asking the same question over and over: *Are your kids deaf or hearing?* Not that I care, because each child is wonderfully unique in their own way. We love them immensely regardless of their hearing status. Perhaps they will remain hearing and someday co-author a book titled *Hearing Again.* Or maybe they'll follow the same pattern my father and I did, losing their hearing later in life. (In which case they could write *Deaf Again: The Next Generation.*) Either way, it doesn't really matter. So long as the kids are happy, I'm happy.

Although the kids were born into Deaf culture and will always be a part of it regardless of their hearing ability, I do recognize that they are still hearing. While they are constantly exposed to sign language—they both developed a remarkable vocabulary of signed words well before they were able to speak—I understand that they also need to interact with other hearing people. I noticed the value of this when Darren first attended Growing Tree Learning Center for daycare while Melanie and I both worked at PSD. Through socialization with his hearing peers, Darren picked up some things that he otherwise would have missed at home.

For example, after a few weeks in daycare, Darren developed an appreciation for music. He loves listening to people singing songs, and he often did this cute little bouncy dance. And one day, after we brought him home from daycare, he spontaneously began clapping his hands. We knew this was something he picked up from hearing culture; after all, we do the "deaf applause" hand wave at home. Such was the value of this that we decided to send Brandon to daycare as well, even after Melanie switched to teaching part-time in the evening.

Ultimately, we believe that it is our kids' right as hearing children to be exposed to hearing peers and role models, even though they're growing up in a primarily deaf environment. We know they will make the best of both worlds and we want them to have the opportunity to learn from each.

Yes, you probably see where this is going. I want to point out that likewise, it is only fair that deaf children get the opportunity to interact with deaf peers and role models. It would be unfair if I kept my children away from other hearing people, and I hope people can understand that it would be equally unfair to keep deaf children away from the Deaf community.

From time to time, I have heard hearing parents express fear that the Deaf community would "steal" their deaf children away from them. This has puzzled me in the past, and now that I have children of my own, it puzzles me even more. After all, I do not fear that hearing culture will "steal" my hearing kids from me. Quite the contrary, I welcome hearing relatives, teachers, and peers into their lives, so that they can have all the more enriching experiences. We all deserve the opportunity to find out who we are. As you can see in this book, it was such an opportunity that turned my life around.

Another unique aspect of deaf parents raising hearing children is the remarkable role of ASL in their lives. Melanie and I hadn't given this much thought at first; with Darren and Brandon, signing with our kids was something we did naturally. Both of them picked up ASL long before they were developmentally able to speak. In a nutshell, they'd already built a significant language base before non-signing hearing kids even uttered their first word. We didn't realize this, but we were giving our kids a head start by wiring their brains for language at a much earlier age. Research has since proven that there are many advantages, including higher IQ, that come out of signing with your baby.

After Lacey was born, it wasn't long before she, too, demonstrated an incredible knack for picking up ASL. By then, the baby sign language frenzy was in full force. There are now countless hearing parents of hearing babies who are using sign language to promote early communication and language development. Although research on this actually started in the 1980s, I believe it was Robert DeNiro's portrayal of a sign language-obsessed grandfather in *Meet the Fockers* in 2004 that ultimately catapulted baby sign language into mainstream consciousness. Its popularity has exploded since then.

Being the scholarly guy that I am, I had to look into this further. I'd taken Darren and Brandon's signing skills for granted, but this time around I wanted to see exactly how Lacey matched up with her non-signing peers. The results startled me. At the tender age of eleven months, Lacey was able to communicate at a level you'd expect from a toddler between the ages of eighteen and twenty-four months. According to *The Baby Book: Everything You Need to Know About Your Baby—From Birth to Age Two* (by William Sears, M.D. and Marsha Sears, R.N., 1993), Lacey was at an age where you'd expect her to utter two-syllable sounds such as "ma-ma" or "da-da" and perhaps associate those sounds with the right person.

Instead, here was eleven-month-old Lacey going "There's the kitty cat," "I want a cookie," "More cookies," "Look, it's Elmo!" and "I want a bath." That's only the tip of the iceberg. Included in her extended vocabulary at that age were words and names such as *Daddy, Mommy, Darren, Brandon, Grandmom, funny, water, baby, The Wiggles, finished, all gone, yes, no, bye-bye, ball, dog, eat, sleep, potty,* and more. She also demonstrated the ability, with her repeated exposure to ASL, to put these words together in multiple-word sentences. In retrospect, Darren and Brandon had done the same thing. They all were conversing—not just saying words, but actually *conversing*—at an age where most kids were just getting past the babbling stage. I found it so amazing that I posted a more in-depth analysis about it on *Deaf Culture Online* (www.deaf-culture-online.com).

And then, a very sensitive issue—signing with your *deaf* baby—was brought up in one of my favorite deaf-related mailing lists. A good friend of mine, MaryAnne Kowalczyk, said it best:

If signing with hearing babies has proven to be so successful, why aren't we encouraged to sign with our deaf babies, the ones who need it the most?

Well-said, MaryAnne. I'm going to step back for a moment and let everyone chew on that thought.

All in all, I'm thrilled to be able to say my household is bilingual. As we continue to grow, we continue to thrive in two worlds with two languages. We're truly blessed.

Often, when people ask me what the turning point in my life was, I tell them about Linda Baine pulling me out of the supermarket and eventually helping me discover something known as *Deaf Pride*. Many people simply do not understand this phenomenon. After all, they ask, how could someone possibly be proud of what, in essence, is nothing more than a disability? On top of that, deafness is a disability that affects communication. It can put an invisible wall between hearing and deaf people. So what's there to be proud of?

If you had asked me this question many years ago, I would have been hard-pressed to come up with an answer. *Deaf Pride?* What Deaf Pride? What about all those times in hearing schools, when I had to give up and simply say, "I don't know," because I couldn't understand the teacher? What about all those times I was made fun of? What about all those times I was put in an audiologist's booth like a guinea pig? What about all those times the speech teachers squeezed my mouth and said, "C'mon, can you say BA-BA-BA?" That's certainly nothing to be proud of. In fact, I was downright embarrassed at times.

That is, embarrassed until I got to join Deaf culture. I may have joined it late, after years of unsuccessfully trying to be like a hearing person, but better late than never. Meeting other deaf peers like myself, sharing similar stories of oppression and ridicule, learning ASL, and seeing other deaf adults succeed has completely changed my attitude. I am no longer ashamed of my deafness. I'm proud of it. I am proud of who I am, proud of what I've overcome, and I am proud of my culture.

Yes, I recognize such a thing as Deaf culture. Some people may be sighing, "Oh no, not that old culture

180

vs. pathology argument." I acknowledge that there are many people out there, even deaf people, who insist that deafness is nothing more than an annoying disability. As my past would indicate, that could certainly be an accurate description. Other people adamantly insist that there is a Deaf culture (emphasizing the capital D), that deafness is not a handicap at all, and that "Deaf people can do anything but hear."

I choose to take somewhat of a middle stance. My own definition is: *Deafness is a disability that is so unique, its very nature causes a culture to emerge from it.* Participation in this culture is voluntary. And I officially enlisted in 1989.

Being a part of this culture has given me a sense of pride. I am no longer alone; I share a language, ASL, with many other people in the Deaf community. I share a history of a struggle that is well documented; not only are there stories related to growing up deaf passed along within the Deaf community, but there are now countless books as well. I enjoy ASL poetry and deaf puns/jokes that cannot be translated into written English; they are unique in that they can only be understood within the framework of ASL. I enjoy attending plays and community events that focus on many deaf issues. I also use a number of deaf mannerisms, of which there are several. For instance, the "deaf applause" cheer (waving one's hands in the air instead of clapping), or a repertoire of visual expressions and signs that relay concepts far more quickly than mere words ever could, and a tendency to be more physically-oriented (i.e. tapping my foot, tapping someone's shoulder, waving, blinking lights, etc., to get someone's attention), and so on.

I can't emphasize enough how much it means to have a sense of belonging. People need to realize that there's a big difference between "fitting in" and "belonging." *Fitting in* is something I did when I immersed myself in the hearing world. Fitting in requires effort. It's exhausting and you can also argue that it's not really genuine

181

because to one degree or the other, it involves trying to win other people's approval. *Belonging,* on the other hand, is a far more rewarding phenomenon where you can kick back, be yourself, and know you are accepted. This is far more authentic and often happens in the presence of one's true peers.

And my true peers *rock.* I bask in pride when I see deaf people becoming more and more successful in the world. There are those who feel that Deaf culture shelters deaf people from the "real world"—but from my perspective, it *strengthens* us and allows us to make the most of both worlds. Participating in a core group such as the Deaf community provides a strong foundation of inner strength and self-esteem that helps people succeed anywhere they want to, including the mainstream. That is, after all, what this whole book is all about.

Indeed, more and more deaf people are getting advanced degrees and becoming doctors, lawyers, administrators, and (ahem) authors. It is a feeling of pride and support that pushes us on. In my case, it was seeing the successful outcome of the Deaf President Now movement that inspired me to transfer to Gallaudet University and to set my goals higher than ever. What really sticks out in my mind is that there once was a time when I never would have thought that any of this could be possible. As the pseudo-hearing child I was so many years ago I had grown accustomed to depending on other people, being lost in the crowd, and accepting limits that others imposed on me (as well as some that I imposed on myself).

Today, however, I stand on my own two feet. So yes, as far as I'm concerned, there is such a thing as Deaf Pride. It exists for me, and it's the spark that changed my life. As one would say in ASL, "Deaf Pride, Pah!" ("Deaf Pride, Finally!")

Epilogue

::

hen I first wrote and published *Deaf Again* in 1997, it was one of the hardest things I'd ever done in my life. Normally, writing a book and having it published is the thrill of a lifetime. But this book was a bit too personal. This was about my family, all the good stuff and the bad stuff. Mostly good stuff, but... the bad stuff was brutally honest. Like many other deaf people with hearing relatives, I have experienced a considerable number of communication difficulties.

It can be a real bummer, something every family with a deaf child should be aware of. And for the deaf children themselves, I wanted to provide something they could relate to—an opportunity to show family and friends this book, an opportunity to say, *"See, that's exactly how I felt."* Incidentally, that is precisely what happened, and I'm happy with the results.

Nonetheless, when the very first shipment of books was fresh off the press, I nearly stopped in my tracks. I couldn't go through with it. Every worse case scenario flashed through my mind. My family was either going to have their feelings hurt, or they were going to be mad as hell. Or both. They would disown me and I would move to a remote cabin somewhere in Switzerland.

After much soul-searching, I decided to go for it with *Deaf Again.* If I was guilty of anything, it was of telling the truth—truth that needed to be heard. My biggest reinforcement came from Lisa Bain, an accomplished writer who has published three books of her own. When I expressed to her my concern about family members feeling bad about certain deaf issues, she smiled knowingly. Then in her own polite and thoughtful way, she asked, "Don't you think they already know?"

She was right. Yes, they already knew. It was never an issue of knowing about deafness; it was about coping with it. There were no answers for my family until they read the book. Immediately, the changes were obvious.

During a small get-together with some hearing friends and relatives, my hearing grandmother caught me struggling to keep up with the conversation. She saw me staring intently at a relative's lips, straining my neck, asking this person to repeat things over and over, and finally just nodding it off when it got too frustrating. Grandmom turned to my mother and said, "He doesn't understand a word, does he?"

At last! She always knew—but today, she *understood*. So much in fact, that at the next major family gathering, she agreed to make arrangements to bring in a sign language interpreter. Awesome! What followed was a major breakthrough.

Three weeks later, we had our first interpreted family gathering. It was with several hearing relatives, three deaf people (my mother, my wife, and myself), and one very competent interpreter. It was nirvana.

Dinner table conversation was no longer a bore. Grandmom was telling a story about how her mother used to keep live fish in the bathtub before preparing them for dinner. My uncle and two other relatives were engaged in a heavy debate about religious pluralism. I watched with fascination. A whole new world had opened up. These strangers at the dinner table had suddenly transformed into very interesting people!

It didn't matter if the deaf relatives were actively involved in the conversation or not. Sometimes we joined in; sometimes we just sat back and enjoyed the show. With the interpreter, we had a new set of ears to let us know what was going on at all times. There was no boredom whatsoever.

The real kicker was a conversation with my cousin

184

Eleanor. A pleasant young woman, Eleanor has always been an interesting person. However, her speech pattern for whatever reason had always been difficult for me to follow. I never realized it until just then, but I had always manipulated our conversations in such a way that it never went beyond the superficial. This was because if we had ever jumped to a brand new topic, I would not have been able to keep up. It's much easier to lip-read, of course, when you know the conversation will stick to "How's the family" and "How's the job."

With the interpreter, though, we took it to a new level. During the discussion on religious issues I was surprised to find myself agreeing with Eleanor several times. From a philosophical standpoint, we were practically twins. Only then, after all these years, did I realize this. To top it all off, I also discovered that she takes an Aikido class and we share a similar interest in the martial arts. I have been a martial artist for several years, most recently becoming involved in Tai Chi and Kempo, yet I had never had such a discussion with Eleanor. I'd had no idea she was into the same thing. We wound up having a great talk, sharing notes about our respective martial arts styles. All of this thanks to the 'terp.

When the evening drew to a close, I checked my watch and did a double take. It was 10:30 p.m. Under the usual circumstances—no interpreter and plenty of boredom—we would have been out of there by 7:30. This time, however, we stayed for the whole duration and got to know my family on a different level. And thus, looking back on *Deaf Again*, there's no doubt about it; it was *deafinitely* worth it.

Introducing another book from the author of Deaf Again!

∷

Anything But Silent

Anything But Silent is a compilation of the most thought-provoking articles by renowned deaf writer Mark Drolsbaugh. With a perfect blend of humor and insight, Drolsbaugh tackles some of the most profound topics in deafness: deaf/hearing relationships, the rift between American Sign Language and English, the hidden world of the hard of hearing, oppression in politics and education, idiosyncrasies of the deaf and hearing, embarrassing moments, and much more. Anything But Silent offers a deaf perspective rarely seen in print — bringing knowing smiles to those familiar with the deaf community and enlightening those who are new to it.

∷

What people are saying about **Anything But Silent:**

"Mark Drolsbaugh is a writer with this amazing ability, magical even, to tell a story that hits home every time. Whether it's about the frustrations or awesome joys unique to the world of deafness and sign language, he pulls in his readers for an eye-opening experience. You're in for a real treat so sit down, get comfortable, and enjoy the ride!"

– *Marvin Miller, Executive Director*
The Laurent Institute

"Anything But Silent so beautifully captures the essence of the deaf community. It's an empowering and entertaining collection of writing that truly shows what it means to be deaf. I know this to be true as a hearing mom having raised two deaf children of my own."

– *Carol Finkle, Founder/Executive Director*
Creative Access

∷

On the Fence:
The Hidden World of the Hard of Hearing

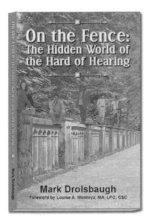

On the Fence: The Hidden World of the Hard of Hearing delivers a rare inside look at a virtually invisible population. *Deaf writer Mark Drolsbaugh, who grew up hard of hearing, has assembled a group of thirty-seven talented writers who share their remarkable stories and poems. Together, they shed light on the hard of hearing experience and what it means to be on the fence—hovering somewhere in between the deaf and hearing worlds.*

..

Topics Include:

* Communication methods and preferences

* Bluffing through work, school, and family events

* The two words hard of hearing people hate to hear

* Hard of hearing CODAs (Children of Deaf Adults)

* Stories from grade school, high school, and college students

* Deaf and late-deafened people who also spent time as "fencers"

* And much, much, more!

Stereotypes are smashed as each writer shares a unique perspective. But don't let the diversity fool you; while no one is the same, deep down we all share one common goal. Find it in *On the Fence: The Hidden World of the Hard of Hearing.*

..

For more information, visit our website at:
www.handwavepublications.com